WOMEN'S
MEDICINE
WAYS

WOMEN'S MEDICINE WAYS

Cross-Cultural Rites of Passage

by
Marcia Starck
with Gynne Stern

The Crossing Press · Freedom, CA 95019

For information on bulk purchases or group discounts for this and other Crossing Press titles, please contact our Special Sales Manager at 800-777-1048.

Library of Congress Cataloging-in Publication-Data

Starck, Marcia.
    Women's medicine ways : cross-cultural rites of passage / by Marcia Starck with Gynne Stern.
        p. cm.
    Includes bibliographical references and index.
    ISBN 0-89594-597-5. -- ISBN 0-89594-596-7 (paper)
    1. Witchcraft. 2. Goddess religion--Rituals. 3. Women--Religious life--Cross-cultural studies. 4. Rites and ceremonies--Cross-cultural studies. I. Stern, Gynne. II. Title.
BF1566.S765 1993
131'.082--dc20
                                                                93-25819
                                                                CIP

Acknowledgments

I wish to thank the following people:

Oh Shinnah, for opening me up to medicine ways and initiating
me into my first moon ceremony.

Grandmother Twylah, for her teachings, support, and information
throughout the years.

Frida Waterhouse, no longer here on the physical plane, for her
spiritual guidance that enabled me to trust and become a
vehicle for higher knowledge.

Gynne Stern, for editing and writing portions of the manuscript.

Rohmana Harris, for the beautiful cover and her inspired art work.

Jenny D'Angelo, my editor, for her care and consideration in
working with the manuscript.

Elaine and John Gill and Brigid Fuller at The Crossing Press,
for all their help and time.

*I dedicate this book
to the FREEDOM
of every woman
in every country
on this planet.*

Contents

Foreword

Women's Medicine Ways—Cross-Cultural Rites of Passage was written several years ago; however, this book did not choose to birth itself until this great year of changes, 1993, the year the planets Uranus and Neptune conjoin in the heavens.

Creating ceremonies for various rites of passage is not a new idea for some of us. But for other women, rituals for entering the crone phase or puberty ceremonies for maidens, is a totally new experience, adding another dimension to their lives.

On the best-seller list this year are books on menopause (a topic barely discussed in public for decades) and on the "wild woman" archetype. New magazines like *Crone Chronicles* are affording older women a vehicle in which to share and communicate their ideas as well as a place in which to publish their creative outpourings.

Politically, 1992 was dubbed the "Year of the Woman." Not only did we increase the number of women in the United States Senate and House of Representatives, but we also voted in a new administration, based on more compassionate feminine principles with a First Lady, Hillary Rodham Clinton, who embodies women's empowerment and who shares the stage equally with her husband, the President. Lunar and solar forces are reunited at this time, and that "sacred marriage" which we all desire within our own beings, is now in the limelight, beaming across our television screens.

Unfortunately, this is only part of the story. The treatment and contempt for women in much of the world is deplorable and difficult for many of us to comprehend when it is being done by other women, women who are uneducated and themselves suffering from poverty and abuse. Only a few days ago did I see this headline in my local newspaper, "Sentencing a daughter to death may be better than condemning her to life as a woman in the Third World." The story was about women in India who kill their girl children, sometimes by pouring scalding chicken soup down their throats, sometimes by strangling them. By making this sacrifice, it is hoped that a boy child, requiring no dowry and who will be able to work and support the family, will be forthcoming. Women in cities have the benefit of amniocentesis which will alert them to the presence of a female fetus and enable them to abort before it comes to term. Even if the girl is allowed her life, she may be sold off later as a prostitute or married off to an abusive husband.

Many Muslim women from Africa and the Near East perform surgeries on their own daughters, clitoridectomies and infibulations, painful procedures with no anesthetics that traumatize these young women and make them victims to the demands and pleasures of the male sex. These are considered important rites of passage, ones that we women in the rest of the world would like to totally eliminate.

With more and more circles of women conducting rituals and sharing together, the channels of communication are becoming greater and spreading so that, in time, we will see the freedom of *all* women.

I offer this book as a gift to every woman so that she might empower herself by participating in ritual at important life passages. The chapters are merely guidelines, stimulating each of us to employ our own creativity and individuality in celebrating our life. May it be so!

Marcia Starck
April 6, 1993
(full moon in Libra)
Santa Fe, N M

Introduction

"Hey, Hey, Hey, Hey, Hey, Ungua, Hey, Hey, Hey, Hey, Ungua . . . ." I rolled over in my sleeping bag and watched the pinks and reds of the dawning day while I listened to my new friend, sister, and teacher, Oh Shinnah, chant the morning invocation. It was spring, 1977. I was with a group (later a clan) of people gathered in Northern California's lush Emerald Valley to learn the Emerald Tablets Meditation. Before coming to this valley, our group fasted for four days and read the ancient Emerald Tablets of Thoth, attributed to Hermes or Thoth. Oh Shinnah, our leader, is Apache, Mohawk, and Scottish. She plays the guitar, sings, works with crystals, and knows many of the ancient mysteries. She calls herself a servant of the medicine.

That first morning our group performed a sunrise tobacco ceremony; each of us saying a prayer to the new day and sprinkling the earth with a pinch of tobacco. We called in the four directions, Earth Mother, and Sky Father to bless us and hear our special prayers. I felt something open deep within myself. I had no name for it, but the feeling was old and familiar, for I was performing an ancient medicine way—one of the timeless rituals to greet the sun, done thousands of times by many peoples all over the world throughout the ages. The ritual was simple: a pinch of tobacco, a fire in the middle of our circle, the calling in of the four directions. Yet, the effect was extremely powerful, connecting us to all our relations on the planet—the sky, the trees, the plants, the birds, the two-leggeds and the many-legged.

To this day, I still continue to go outside every morning wherever I am and offer my prayers to the directions, to Earth Mother and Sky Father, and bless the new day. I have scattered tobacco in downtown Chicago, in the high Sierras, and on the beaches of Hawaii.

After spending that weekend in the Emerald Valley, I decided to continue learning other ceremonies— a women's moon ceremony, the earth renewal ceremony done at Winter Solstice, and Blessingways. I was also introduced to the sweat lodge and the Way of the Pipe, to the Native American church, and the use of the drum, rattle, and talking stick. All of these ceremonies and rituals harked back to ancient ways of connecting with the Great Mystery and honoring the Earth Mother.

When I moved from the San Francisco Bay Area to the Sierra foothills in 1985, I couldn't find a group working with ancient medicine ways, so I began to organize and lead ceremonies with the help of a few others doing similar ritual work. Whenever we did an equinox, solstice, or moon ceremony, many participants felt they received a deep healing. Women especially seemed to need the moon rituals to connect them to Earth Mother and help heal wounds inflicted by a society dominated by masculine and linear values. I found ritual to have a stronger healing effect than individual counseling sessions. In rituals, participants could contact higher states, connect to the universal energy, and let go of old patterns that were no longer effective. People were changed afterwards, and the changes lasted.

Slowly, it became obvious to me that women, particularly those who worked with or were heavily involved in family commitments, needed a habitual way to become aware of the natural rhythms of their bodies and the connection their bodies had to the rhythms of the universe. I began to devise ceremonies for women that would help them honor the important stages of their lives.

When I returned to the Bay Area in late 1986, I heard a tape on the Crone that stimulated me to conceive a ritual for menopausal women which I called a Crone Rite of Passage. A few friends and I were excited by the idea of having a ritual to celebrate a transition which women today often regard as a crisis point—a time of lost youthfulness preceded by a period of hot flashes and other uncomfortable physical changes. Women aren't given the opportunity to understand the positive aspects of "the change of life." I felt Isis Oasis Retreat Center in California's wine country was the ideal site to hold the workshop. The retreat center, just outside of the tiny town of Geyserville, has a small menagerie of wild animals and exotic birds who are allowed to range freely throughout the grounds. One of the buildings, a delicate, brilliantly white Egyptian temple, was consecrated to the goddess Isis. Here at this center, already named for the Goddess, twenty women spent two days attending workshops, making costumes and masks for a Hallows Eve celebration, dancing and drumming, and finally undergoing a rebirth ritual in which each woman chose a new name symbolic of her status as an elder of society and a wise woman.

Also, for some years, I had been hearing about the renewed interest in the Goddess. I had been familiar since childhood with many of the mythological goddesses, particularly those in the Greco-Roman and Egyptian traditions, and I had friends in covens who performed Wiccan ceremonies. As I began to study Wiccan ritual, I was fascinated by how similar Wiccan ceremonies were to those from Native American cultures.

In Wiccan tradition, the Goddess in some form is always the principal deity. In the early '70s, the Gaia hypothesis (a scientific theory which posits the planet earth as a living, breathing organism who reacts to her surroundings in a manner similar to other living beings) caused renewed interest in the Earth Mother, the Goddess, and eco-feminism. Wiccan practices, kept alive by many generations of witches, wise women, seers, and healers, had helped the survival of paganism, which remained buried beneath the Christian, Judaic, and Islamic traditions. Paganism is the belief in the old gods and goddesses who represent natural forces or archetypes. Much of what is pictorial or colorful in Catholicism, for example, came from the need to satisfy the country folk and peasants with reminders of their old deities, now called by new names and worshipped at different shrines. Protestantism, with its emphasis on the Word as expressed in the Bible, and Judaism, with its taboo against any depiction of God, went farther in removing the newer, god-centered religions from their ancient pagan base.

All modern religions—the various forms of Christianity, Judaism, Hinduism, Buddhism, Islam—have turned away from the practices and rituals of paganism, which were based on the movements of the sun, moon, and stars (even though the religious calendars of both Judaism and Islam still are based on the lunar calendar). Pagan religions have been called "pantheistic" because they hold that the divine force is present in all of nature. Pantheism contradicts the notion of the mind/body split so prominent in Western philosophy.

Perhaps the feminist movement in the '60s and '70s aroused the spirit of the Goddess and caused women to look for their philosophic and spiritual roots in civilizations where the Goddess was the primary deity. Scholars and archaeologists began to study prehistoric cultures to discover the nature and structure of societies where women ruled. The invaluable research of Marija Gimbutas helped relate ancient art and artifacts in Europe and the Near East to the very early religions of the Goddess and prehistoric matrilineal cultures. Gimbutas' work had been preceded by many decades by Jane Ellen Harrison's *Prolegomena to the Greek Religion.* Harrison, who studied the mythology of Ancient Greece and the Cyclades, also concluded that a strong matrilineal culture underlay the later worship of the sky gods, but her work, although well-known to scholars, never achieved popular distribution due to the prejudices of her time. Merlin Stone's *When God Was a Woman* provided another popular work which delineated the ancient goddess religions and showed their survival into the present. Currently, many scholars and writers on women's spirituality agree that the Goddess has been in hiding, in her "dark moon phase," for thousands of years and has recently reappeared. With the reappearance of the Goddess, strong feminine energy can return to the planet.

In Western countries, nature (and her representative, woman), originally a force to be worshipped and understood, has become something to be controlled and suppressed. Nature and woman have two faces. One is beautiful, gentle, and life-giving. It is this face of woman and nature that has been celebrated in Western art for the past 2000 years. The other face is terrifying. When the beautiful face of woman becomes alluring (luring man to destruction or forgetfulness by its charm), when woman's body in response to her monthly cycle bleeds or when she is observed in the bloody agony of childbirth or creation, her aspect becomes as fearsome as the sandstorm in the desert, the eruption of a volcano, or the refusal of the Nile to flood its banks in the spring. Early women and men knew the value of watching nature. They conducted ceremonies and rituals to court and propitiate her. The culture of the sky god, with its emphasis on the sword, the pen, the paint brush, the sculptor's tool, or the surgeon's scalpel tried to transform and control what was perceived as horrible in nature into something beautiful, manageable, and ordered. But the old feminine earth religion was never completely suppressed, nor is modern science capable of preventing the eruptions of nature or eliminating the man-made horrors of warfare and pollution.

Wicca, the term for various pagan or magical groups in Western culture, is the root of the word "wake" or "awake." Wicca is a watching and a watching over; a ceremonial acknowledgment of the cyclical changing of the heavens and an understanding that the movement of the earth and the heavenly bodies affect the affairs and progress of humankind.

Today women all over the planet seek to connect with their feminine energy; they are beginning to understand that masculine energy—often known as science, art, and religion—if relied on exclusively, is inadequate and debilitating for both sexes. They are also discovering the power of using ritual to honor the natural cycles of their lives which parallel the life of the Great Mother, the Earth.

The more I observe the growing interest in ritual and in the ways of earlier peoples who lived more closely with the earth, the more I seek information about goddesses from different cultures, what these goddesses represented, and their function in ritual. Merlin Stone's book, *Ancient Mirrors of Womanhood*, is a treasure of information on fertility, virgin, animal, mother, crone, and funerary goddesses from all over the world.

Of particular interest to me have been the dark goddesses, those goddesses who represent the repressed parts of nature—the wild, unruly, freedom-loving goddesses—and those who deal with death and the mysteries. Some examples are: Kali, creatress and destroyer from India; Pele, Hawaiian goddess of the erupting volcano; Hecate of Greece, who stands at the crossroads greeting travelers; Inanna and Ereshkigal, the Sumerian sister goddesses—one forced to live in the underworld, the other who chose to visit there; the Hebrew Lilith, banished to the wilderness because she refused to lie beneath Adam; Oya, the African goddess in charge of departed souls; Sekhmet, the Egyptian lion-headed goddess who slaughtered humans and drank their blood; the Moorigan from Celtic mythology, who as the destructive crone, Macha, delighted at spilled blood; and Hella, the Scandinavian goddess who ruled over the land of the dead. These goddesses are all precursors and reflections of the Black Madonna, the evil woman, the whore, the Magdalene, as opposed to the white virginal Madonna revered by Christianity. Here we come across another fear universal to humankind—that of black or darkness. Black, since it represents night and the unknown, is thought of as evil, while white, which designates the clarity of day, stands for the good. Just as the fear of the incalculability of nature has been transferred to a desire to suppress and dishonor women, so the fear of blackness has been transferred to people with black or dark skin. These fears are atavistic ones and not easily eradicated.

When I work with the "dark goddesses" in ritual, I have seen both men and women experience deep transformation. They feel the anger, fear, and wildness within themselves rather than transferring these emotions onto other persons or things; they start to realize that both dark and light are a part of the natural order, and that the dark part does not need to be suppressed or denied.

Native American cultures, in both North and South America, also have goddesses who portray certain qualities that help us in ritual. Changing Woman (Estsan Atlehi) is the Navajo Earth Mother and anthropomorphic deity celebrated in many Navajo and Apache rituals, as is the Pueblo Spider Grandmother who created the universe. White Buffalo Woman, who brought the pipe of peace to humanity, appears in Lakota Sioux legends as well as those of other Plains tribes. In South and Central America, goddesses such as Coatlicue, Aztec Mother Goddess; Ix Chel, Mayan Moon Goddess; and Chicomecoatl, the Great Corn Mother of the Aztecs, are prevalent in myth and ceremony.

The use of goddesses in present-day ritual helps women to personify certain qualities and energies. When women create masks and dress as the goddesses, they are enabled to work "magical" changes in their lives. When a woman makes an altar in her home or garden and decorates this altar with meaningful objects, she can start to manifest her desires in the world. As she follows the lunar calendar through the year, beginning with the Winter Solstice, and celebrating a month of twenty-eight days, rather than the usual thirty or thirty-one of the solar calendar, she connects the book of days and seasons to the rhythms of her own body.

Modern women, without a tribal structure, or often even a family structure and without the bolstering of a tightly knit society with seasonal celebrations and rituals, are in the position of needing to draw from the past—from Native American traditions, from the pagan traditions of Europe, from the Far East, from African tribal rituals, and from Australian aboriginal rites. Partaking in these rituals points to ways of finding collective empowerment for women.

As women, we desire to celebrate and make meaningful each step on our road of life, from birth to crossing over. We want to know how to share these events with our friends and relations so that they will catalyze new growth within our circles and our community. We feel the importance of being awake to each step of the process of human female life in a deep and complete way so that we might be more watchful of the responses of nature and how our rhythms coincide with hers.

In this book I have taken a cross-cultural approach to ritual because I feel that although certain rituals and goddesses are endemic to the societies in which they originated, they are not foreign in concept to women today in the Western world. For example, all North American women of whatever ethnic background, have been brought up in the predominant European culture, with its emphasis on the importance of business and material success, its disparagement of women, and its glorification of the male. Ancient Wiccan ceremonies help women reclaim a past when women were the watchers, guardians, and interpreters of nature, and where the natural order was respected by both sexes. Similarly, everyone living in the United States is haunted by the spirit of those native peoples whom the European settlers so ruthlessly wiped out as they forged across the country toward the Pacific Ocean. These spirits still reside in the land and need to be understood and called on.

One of the highlights of the latter part of this century is the global movement of peoples. As more and more immigrants and visitors come to North America from the Far East, we see a resurgence of interest in Eastern philosophy. Thirty years ago the philosophy sections of most bookstores were filled with the works of Plato, Kant, Kierkegaard, and Nietzsche. Today, one is far more likely to encounter Lao Tze, Rumi, Krishnamurti, and Suzuki. As East and West mingle, we need to incorporate into our rituals the goddesses as well as ancient earth lore and science of the Far and Near East.

This book, then, is an attempt to present women's medicine ways from many ancient cultures as ideas and inspiration to create rituals and ceremonies in keeping with our own time and intentions. Rites of passage ceremonies are suggested for each of the important stages on our path, with the hope that every woman will add her own creations and embellishments. Many of the rituals in this book for the lunations and seasonal cycles such as the equinox, solstice, and cross-quarter days are appropriate for men as well as women. However, there are special rituals for birth, puberty, menopause, and moon ceremonies that are strictly women's medicine ways and should not be practiced by men. Men, too, have their medicine ceremonies. I write from the point of view of a woman who conducts ceremonies for women's mysteries, but I also have conducted joint ceremonies for men and women. I believe it is important for women and men to have their own ceremonies and then to come together for mutual rituals. Sharing ceremonies with men helps women in the inner or sacred marriage of the female and male so that the contact between the earth and the sky is a loving marriage and not the battleground that often exists. The Goddess and the God, Mother Earth and Father Sky, live within each of us.

My wish is that this book will guide each reader into the depths of her own being and help her realize the joy of her own process. May you walk in beauty; may the earth breathe in peace.

Medicine Ways and Rituals

What is a medicine way? How can we perform medicine ways that are meaningful today?

A medicine way is a form of healing, a ritualized action that we perform with conscious intent. In a sense, a medicine way is a method of living in the world so that all of our actions from such ordinary daily tasks as scrubbing the kitchen floor to a once in a lifetime ceremony honoring the onset of puberty are performed as rituals. Medicine ways and rituals help us change our consciousness and incorporate the Goddess/God within ourselves.

Women have always been caretakers and providers; they birth their children, feed them, and tend them when they are ill. At the end of life, women are the ones who customarily gather to help with crossing over. Women nurture both their physiological children and all of humankind. The feminine mode operates in an intuitive, feeling way and is not exclusive to the female sex; it is shared by men in varying degrees just as a more traditionally masculine approach to life is followed by many females, particularly in our present society. The masculine mode is authoritative, rigid, dictatorial, and hierarchical, operating on reason and logic rather than feeling and intuition. Most of us have grown up under this patriarchal mode of consciousness and have to work to break away from certain restrictive patterns of thinking and acting. Male thinking tends to make nature conform to a sense of order, while women want to observe and honor her. Here medicine ways and ritual are particularly helpful because they allow women to connect with and honor the cyclical rhythms of both nature and her own physical life.

From the very beginnings of civilization, rituals have been performed to align our energies with the natural and cosmic forces that surround us, to make us aware that we are part of a larger whole, and that our thoughts, actions, and feelings influence those around us and the environment. The ancients and so-called "primitive" peoples prayed for rain in times of drought, blessed the seeds they planted so that they might have enough food for the tribe, and tried to communicate with other living creatures so that all could live in harmony on the earth. The earth was respected and cherished as mother, nurturer, goddess—the one who gives life and takes it away.

In the Near East and Europe, the growth of newer god-centered religions gradually obscured earlier pagan nature cults and rituals and caused those who still performed them to go into hiding. Ceremonies designed to thank and bless the Goddess were forced underground or else hidden within the dominant religion (for example, the cult of the Virgin Mary within the Catholic Church). Knowledge of earlier rituals became *occult* (or hidden) and *esoteric* (known to only a few devotees). Astrology, or divination by observation of the stars, and alchemy, the transmutation of the base metals into spiritual gold, became esoteric disciplines practiced by the few and often condemned as blasphemous by the church or subversive by the state.

During certain periods of history and in certain places, women were burned for their knowledge of natural healing; and their medicines, superior to those in common usage, were thought to be products of the devil. Fear suppressed the transmission of their knowledge; and the Goddess herself went into hiding. Particularly in the last three hundred years, the emphasis on "scientific" or "empiric" thinking, the rise of the city, the movement of peoples away from nature, and the continuing hostility of most established churches have driven the earlier "natural" knowledge further and further from public consciousness. Even today with (or perhaps in response to) the general interest in the Gaia hypothesis and the worldwide recurrence of the study of astrology, herbology, and other esoteric and natural practices, the Catholic Church has spoken out against meditation and other spiritual disciplines which empower individuals to follow their own thinking and reconnect with ancient ways.

Places for Ritual—Altars

The places where we perform ceremonies and rituals are sacred spots, whether small altars in the home, outdoor circles made of stones, or majestic "sacred spots" found at one of the great beauty places of nature.

It is important to create altars and ritual places wherever we are. We can do this in a simple way by placing feathers, herbs or flowers, sage or cedar, incense, or pictures of medicine people, goddesses, ancestors or other significant persons, in each of the four directions. Creating a special place with special objects will bring in the vibratory energy we want to perform the ritual. In Wicca, the altar is often created in the form of a pentacle. The pentacle has five directions: center at the top which represents spirit, east to the right which is air, south just below center representing fire, west to the left representing water, and north or earth at the bottom. The objects used in each direction are symbolic of the energy of that element. When the altar is not shaped like a pentacle, spirit or center is often in the middle of the altar and may be symbolized by a cauldron (to indicate an emergence from the womb) or by crystal balls, giant crystals, or a goddess figure. For east or air, the *athame* (or sword) is used, although in feminist Wiccan circles the sword has been replaced by the wand. Bird feathers or symbols of birds are also often used for east. South or fire is usually represented by a candle or a crystal wand. Candles are always placed somewhere on the altar, and their color might be symbolic of the ritual conducted. West, water, is represented by a cup or chalice, a nurturing healing vehicle. Sea shells or other objects from the sea are often used as well. North, the direction symbolizing the earth element, is often represented by a crystal or rock, a bowl of soil or salt. Traditional Wicca uses the pentacle or five-pointed star to represent earth. The pentacle is the symbol used to designate membership in a coven (an initiated group of people who work together in conducting ritual). The symbols used in the Tarot are connected to Wiccan practice. In Tarot, air is represented by swords to show the cutting power of the intellect; the creativity of fire is indicated by wands; water by the cup; and earth by the pentacle. These elements and their symbols also occur in astrology, pointing to the universal and archetypal nature of certain symbols.

Creating an altar is important before beginning a ritual, regardless of whether the ritual is outdoors where the altar may be placed at the center of the circle, or indoors where the altar could be made in a bedroom or near the fireplace. Specific medicine ways as the Blessingway ceremony are often done around the bed where a mother will give birth.

Henges and Medicine Wheels

Ancient peoples built *henges* and medicine wheels on their land. Henges are groups of stones placed to observe the changing relationships of sky and earth through various seasons. If we chart these relationships, we may also see changes taking place within us. Most henges are built so that the sun's rays at sunset hit the top of the stone. Ideally, the sunset point

should be seen at either the Summer or Winter Solstice or both. A good book to consult when building a henge is *Sun Angles for Design* by Robert T. Bennett (Balla Cynwood, PA, 1978).

If a piece of land is used often, building a medicine wheel on it enhances the ceremonies that are done there. *Medicine* means "spiritual" and *wheel* means "energy," so a *medicine wheel* is a center of "spiritual energy." Many groups, especially Wiccan groups, begin a ritual by casting a circle, or wheel.

The circle is the basis of the medicine wheel; the circle shows the continuity of all creation while enclosing only one portion of space. A medicine wheel is a mandala for beginning a sacred relationship with all of nature; it is a tool for teaching us where we are in our own evolution as we perceive our relationships with the four directions—with the rocks, birds, animals, and plants. Often set up at the place where the first light strikes, the medicine wheel usually contains at least twelve stones. A large center stone represents the center of the universe, the Goddess, Earth Mother, or Great Mystery. Each person building the medicine wheel smudges (purifying through the burning of sage, cedar, and sweetgrass placed in an abalone shell) herself and the stones that she places around the edge. Often stones are placed in the east first, sometimes in the south, and sometimes in another direction if the medicine wheel has a special focus; for example, a healing wheel might start in the west. Prayers are made to the direction where the stones are placed. Once the stones are set, plants or herbs may be placed in the directions, feathers of certain birds, skulls of animals, crystals and gemstones, as well as statues and pictures of goddesses and medicine women. Here are some guidelines for ceremonies. Chapter 2 on moon cycles will offer more comprehensive suggestions for what to use for each different moon cycle.

EAST

Animals	eagle, hawk, deer
Plants	gold and yellow flowers; herbs for illumination and insight such as gota kola, which sharpens the mind
Minerals	amber, topaz, citrine quartz, jasper
Goddesses	Athena, Spider Woman

SOUTH

Animals	mouse, coyote, tiger, lion
Plants	red and orange flowers; herbs that warm the body such as red clover, cayenne, cinnamon
Minerals	carnelian, bloodstone, ruby, garnet
Goddesses	Pele, Brigit (Goddess of the Inner Flame), Sekhmet (Lion Goddess)

WEST

Animals	bear, jaguar, snake, dolphin, owl
Plants	blue and purple flowers; herbs that increase psychic sensitivity such as mugwort
Minerals	moonstone, opal, pearl, smoky quartz, black onyx, obsidian, amethyst, flourite
Goddesses	Inanna/Ereshkigal, Hecate, Kali, Medusa, Cerridwyn, and goddesses of transformation

NORTH

Animals	buffalo, wolf
Plants	all kinds of green herbs, trees such as pine, oak, redwood, eucalyptus that bring authority and wisdom
Minerals	malachite, emerald, turquoise, chrysocolla for the earth and grounding
Goddesses	earth goddesses: White Buffalo Woman, Demeter, Isis, Ishtar, Ceres, Gaia, Oshun

Specific medicine ways start at various places on the wheel. For example, puberty ceremonies often start in the east; crone and medicine woman rituals in the north. Healing ceremonies and rites of passage for death take place in the west, home of the setting sun. Marriage ceremonies usually begin in the south, the place of warmth, faith, the flowering stick, and the open heart.

Another way of using the medicine wheel is by using each of the twelve places on it as a step or lesson on one's spiritual path. These twelve places may be seen as the twelve astrological signs or the cycle of the twelve months of the year. Each has its unique qualities and attributes.

In the east we start with Spring Equinox, when the days and nights are equal; the astrological sign is Aries—a time of new life, new beginnings, and lessons around the self and initiation. If we are beginning some new project, a new relationship, a creative venture, we are in the Aries phase. Building and grounding are symbolic of the Taurus phase; it is time to establish ourselves on earth, to make our foundations solid. In the Gemini phase we learn to communicate our thoughts and feelings, to work with each other and to share.

The south brings the time of the Summer Solstice. Cancer offers the lesson of nurturing and mothering; the protection of our families and clans. Leo brings in creative ability and leadership. (Care must be taken in the Leo phase not to get stuck in one's individual ego or become overambitious or proud, because Leo is the place of the open and valiant heart.) Virgo teaches discrimination, sorting the wheat from the chaff, as well as service to humanity.

Libra, bringing in the Fall Equinox, exemplifies the scales of balance, allowing us to work in partnership and share with another. Scorpio deals with the transformation of energies, the process of deep change—death and regeneration. The sting of the scorpion, jealous and envious feelings, can become transmuted into the dove of peace or the high aspiration of the eagle. Sagittarius develops the breadth of wisdom and philosophical understanding of events.

In Capricorn, with the Winter Solstice, we assume responsibility in the world and learn to become disciplined; to organize and work in groups. Aquarius brings us a concern for humanity and human causes, engendering a spirit of helping and working in community. Pisces, the last place on the wheel, teaches us spiritual service and sacrifice, and enables us to perceive the mysticism and poetry in all things.

Creating Sacred Space

We do not need to have a medicine wheel or henge in order to create a sacred space. It is important that group rituals be performed in a circle because the circle contains the energy and sets the boundaries of ritual space. Once the circle is formed, no one may leave or enter except for small children. All personal emotions—anger, jealousy, animosity—are left outside the circle. We call in our higher selves when in ritual and let go of personality consciousness. The circle is the container for the sacred space and for working with the higher energies: the ancestors, animal spirits, and goddesses that one invokes during ritual.

In the African tradition, the sacred space is sprinkled with water after it is smudged. The priestess sprinkles the floor with water in three lines leading from the entrance of the temple, if there is one, to the center of the circle. This creates three rivers. Then the insignia of the spirits is drawn on the ground with cornmeal. (Luisah Teish reports these ways as used in Haiti and similar ones in Africa, Brazil, Cuba, and New Orleans.)[1]

In the Wiccan tradition, the High Priestess casts the circle with an athame, wand, or long leafy branch. She actually traces the circumference of the circle with her wand or athame as everyone visualizes the circle being created.[2] She moves in a clockwise direction from left to right, as this is the direction of invoking.[3] In Native American tradition, the circle is formed around a fire or altar and then becomes sacred space. Sometimes a ring of cornmeal is also sprinkled around the boundaries of the circle. Some Native American tribes go around the circle clockwise and everything is passed clockwise including tobacco for prayers, medicine bundles, and talking sticks. Other tribal practices go counterclockwise, especially for rituals that are for cleansing and healing. Counterclockwise symbolizes the moon, the inner intuitive energy, whereas clockwise symbolizes the sun, the outer logical energy. Many tribes use both directions, depending on the ceremony.

Cleansing and Smudging

Before coming to a ritual, each woman does her own form of cleansing, both physical and spiritual. For some this may involve taking a bath before putting on special clothes; others may meditate deeply for several days beforehand in order to understand clearly what their intentions are in doing the ritual. For very intense ceremonies, some women will spend several days fasting and purifying. Sometimes, simple hand washing will suffice. It all depends upon the type of ritual.

At the circle everyone is smudged or cleansed (the area itself is cleansed before the altar and circle are set up) by burning some sage, cedar, and sweetgrass and purifying each person's aura with the smoke. Some groups or tribes prefer sage because it is known to have more of a cleansing effect than cedar; cedar is thought to bring in new energy rather than cleanse old energy. (This was shared with me by a Native American elder.) However, other medicine teachers say that it depends where one lives and what is available. Tribes living in the Southwest tended to use sage because it grows readily in desert areas. Tribes on the Northwest coast tended more towards cedar. As for sweetgrass, it has been traditionally associated with women's medicine, though it is now used by both sexes in their ritual. It is obtainable in braids from many distributors of Native American supplies. Both cedar and sage are available dried as well as in smudge sticks, where the dried plants have been tied together. One Native American elder shared with me that it is preferable not to use both cedar and sage in the same smudge stick, because they have different energies. In many rituals that I have conducted we have intentionally used cedar for smudging because so many have been allergic or sensitive to the smell of sage, which can be very strong. There are other types of incense used in the Wiccan tradition. Often just a few drops of water or salt water are sprinkled on each woman's heart chakra, especially if there are women who tend to be allergic to the smoke.

One or two women may go around the circle smudging everyone, or the sage, cedar, or smudge stick can be passed with an abalone shell and feather so that each woman can smudge herself or the woman next to her in the circle. In smudging one passes the smoke over the front and back of her body, hitting all the chakra areas. The smudging cleanses any negative energies or old emotions that had accumulated before the ritual. Smudging also signifies the entering of ritual space and time and allows each woman the time to go deeply within and enter the place between the worlds where ritual takes place.

The room may be also be sprinkled with a combination of oil and water. Luisah Teish mentions using a plant mister to spray the room; she suggests adding a little rum or anisette (for spirit) to pure water.[4]

Calling in the Directions and Elements

Most medicine ceremonies and rituals work with four or six directions: east, south, west, north, above, and below. Native American tribes call above and below

"Sky Father" and "Earth Mother"; in Wicca the center of the circle is used to represent spirit or ether as a fifth element. Sometimes the Goddess is called in or the Goddess and God. The directions are usually called in by the person leading the ceremony, although sometimes a different person calls in each direction. Directions may be called in silently or with words. Native American tradition often uses the rattle with or without words.

Ritualists practicing Wicca start either with the east or center. In Native American practices, some tribes start with the east, the new day, and others begin at south, the place of childhood, warmth, and passion. Rituals from the African diaspora start with center. The High Priestess holds a chalice of water or some other object to represent spirit. She asks the gatekeeper to open the door between the physical and spiritual worlds and to awaken the forces from the other world. She then calls in east, south, west, and north.[5]

The east is the place of dawn, sunrise, and new beginnings. It is a place of illumination and vision and has often been associated with the eagle, who flies the highest of all the birds and is the messenger of spirit. The golden eagle is symbolic of the sunrise, the beginning of wisdom, and a new day. East represents spring, the Spring Equinox when day and night are equal. It represents birth, the beginning of all life when plants and animals sing and rejoice, when humans celebrate the end of the long winter and the cold. East is symbolized by the butterfly coming forth from the chrysalis, the shoots of flowers sticking their necks through the dirt. In the east we manifest the wisdom gained in the north from our solitude in the long winter months and from our ancestors who have gone to their rest in the north. The east is usually associated with the element air, which is breath, the beginnings of life and in-spir-a-tion (to breathe in). (Some Native American tribes associate the element fire with east, probably because of the fiery sun that rises at dawn; they attribute air to north where the cold winds blow.) An eagle feather or another bird's feather is often placed on the altar to represent east.

The south is high noon, the warmth of the sun, the intensity and exuberance of puberty and adolescence. Summer Solstice marks a time of the longest day and shortest night; a time of outdoor celebration and all night fires. In the south we experience the innocence of youth; and with the flowering stick, the flowering of our intuitive nature. In the south we test our faith in the intuitive process. The mouse is often associated with the south, as the mouse represents innocence and trust in the ways of the heart. Though the opening of the heart may be fiery and volcanic, as is the heat of the south, it is also a step in our trusting to the love and warmth that flows through it. Coyote, the trickster is often represented in the south, as coyote tricks us into growth, into learning, even when this is a painful process. The heat of love can burn the heart, and sometimes when we go too near the flames of the south, we withdraw and turn inward. The element of south is fire, the fire of purification and growth. A candle is often placed in the south to represent fire. (Native American tribes who associate fire with east, associate earth with south.)

West is the place of sunset, the time of transition between the day force and the night force, the time when we come into our middle years and begin to look deeply within. Autumn Equinox, when the day and night are again equal, prepares us for the winter and darkness ahead. We can now look at the dark places within our psyches and begin to heal; we have time for introspection and inner growth. The black bear symbolizes west; the bear is warm, nurturing, and healing. The black bear represents the healing of the dark places within each of us. (Often Native American sweat lodges face the west, the direction of healing). Autumn is also a time of harvest; in our middle years we harvest the experiences of our youth and we integrate these fruits deeper into the core of wisdom. Water is the element associated with the west; the waters of Grandmother Ocean cleanse and purify our spirits while removing any physical blocks as we make our journey inward. We often put some water in a vessel or pitcher on the altar to symbolize west.

North is evening, darkness, the place of the elders and ancient ones. When we arrive at north, we have come into the age of wisdom. Winter Solstice marks the time of the longest nights and shortest days, but it also marks the time when the sun begins to increase in strength, so we are celebrating a return of the light. (The light is a symbol of wisdom). North brings cold and snow, heavy winds and winter storms. The buffalo symbolizes the north; the buffalo is a repository of wisdom and knowledge, an animal associated with the Giveaway, as the buffalo provided food and warm clothing. White Buffalo Woman, who brought the pipe of peace to Native Americans, is also associated with this direction. (White is the color of purity and of life renewal). The element earth usually represents the north; some cornmeal or a crystal on our altar symbolizes this direction. (Some Native American tribes associate air with north.)

Prayer for Calling in Directions

To the East, the home of the golden eagle and the rising sun,

To the South, the land of intuition and innocence,

To the West, the home of the black bear and introspection,

To the North, the land of the buffalo, of rain, snow, wisdom, and purity.

A confirmation is often used after prayers such as "Blessed Be" or "Ho" (Native American) or "Modupe" (Yoruba for "thank you").

The prayer for calling in directions may be spoken, sung, spoken with rattles, voiced silently, or combined with other personal prayers to the four directions. In our women's lodge we also call in Earth Mother and Sky Father, and as the seventh direction, we call in the Goddess.

Another variation on the directions is to call in four goddesses—one for each direction. The goddesses used for each direction would depend upon the type of ritual enacted.

East	Spider Woman (Native America); Athena (Greece); Lilith (Hebrew); Aido Hwedo (Haiti).
South	Pele (Hawaii); Oya (Africa); Amaterasu (Japan); Sun Woman (Native America); Hestia (Greece); Vesta (Rome); Brigit (Ireland), Sekhmet (Egypt).
West	Changing Woman (Native America); Hecate (Greece); Kali (India); Inanna/Ereshkigal (Sumeria); Medusa (Africa).
North	White Buffalo Woman (Native American); Oshun (Africa); Sedna (Inuit); Demeter (Greece); Isis (Egypt); Ishtar (Middle East).
For Spirit or Center	The Great Mother is called in her forms as Gaia, Copper Woman, Isis, or Mawu.

At the completion of the ritual, the directions and elements are thanked, either individually, with each direction thanked and then dismissed, or thanks may be given to all the directions, ancestors, elders, and spirits who have been present.

Ritual Clothing

Certain clothing is usually set aside for rituals so that the vibration of the clothing is special and becomes more special each time it is used. Special clothing may include a ritual robe, a shawl, a strand of beads (that also can be worn with street clothes when one wants a certain vibration present). Clothing may be made for ritual use with individual totems, such as animals, birds, plants, or other symbols. Consider making a vest, a jacket, or a robe that carries the symbols of your special medicine. It will enhance the quality of the ceremony you are performing.

In many tribal cultures, special dresses made for the marriage ceremony are handed down for generations. They often have elaborate beadwork and certain patterns symbolic of the type of ceremony for which the dress is being worn. Sometimes a girl makes a special dress at the time of her first menstruation, and this robe is then worn at many of her important rites of passage. In some Native American cultures, special moccasins with beadwork are also made for these ceremonies.

Several years ago, a friend offered to sew for me in exchange for a consultation. I hadn't previously thought of how I wanted my ritual jacket to look, but in shopping for materials, I found just the right material. I then decided to have her make an Eagle Woman jacket, using the special design on my shield. An artist sister of mine helped me paint the design onto a piece of leather, and another friend helped me sew the piece onto the back of the jacket. Not only did I have my special medicine on the jacket, but also the energy of three good friends.

Ritual Objects

Ritual objects that stay with a group and carry the group's vibrations are an integral part of medicine ways. Ritual objects include medicine bags, feather fans, personal and group shields, drums, rattles, pipes, wands, and a group talking stick.

Medicine Bags

A personal medicine bag is essential for each woman who is walking a medicine path. It is nice to make a medicine bag oneself or to be given one as a gift. Medicine bags may be made from many kinds of materials. Leather bags are common and often have bead work on them. Other materials also work well. One can sew designs on the bag or embroider a specific totem (an animal, bird, plant or special symbol) that is meaningful. In the bag, each person often puts crystals, dried herbs, feathers from birds that are special to her, stones, sea shells, or anything else one is given or finds in nature that has particular significance. Often the ashes from sacred fires are put in a small container that is placed in the medicine bag.

Group medicine bags are made as well, especially when a group is bonding together as a lodge, coven, clan, tribe, or during an important ceremony such as a moon ceremony. Objects in a group medicine bag might include some general things as cornmeal, tobacco, or a crystal, as well as individual contributions from each woman. When our women's lodge exchanged medicine bundles with another lodge, one woman put in some blue corn seeds that had been soaked in her menstrual blood. If a bag is made during a ritual, the ashes from the sacred fire should be included.

Feather Fans

Feather fans are important for smudging and for bringing in the spirits. Feathers are messengers from the birds and represent the element air. They direct energies to us and communicate to us. A fan can have one feather or many. Often a solitary eagle feather is used for smudging; it may have beads on the end of it or a tie wrapped around it. I have seen fans made from hawk feathers, turkey feathers, and brilliant green parrot feathers. For certain magical rituals or ceremonies involving the Dark Goddess, owl feathers are used. Owls are associated with the night and wisdom. They are feared by certain tribal cultures and held in awe. I have a special eagle feather, given to me by another medicine teacher, that I use for smudging. I also have a wonderful green parrot feather fan from Peru. When I first saw the parrot fan, I knew immediately it was mine and so did the man selling it because he let me have it very cheaply. When I conduct Crone Rites of Passage or Dark Goddess ceremonies, I use my owl feathers, which were given to me by a special friend when I moved to a new area a few years ago. Different feathers carry different energies and it is good to have several feather fans for different purposes. If you are in a women's lodge or coven, try making your own feather fans.

Personal and Group Shields

A shield is used for personal psychic protection and empowerment; it contains the symbols of one's power animals, plants, birds, or actual parts such as feathers, animal fur or hair, dried herbs, and crystals. A shield is a circle and is made from a hoop covered with wood or cloth. Sometimes shields are painted, sometimes the objects are fastened on with glue or sewn on with needle and thread. If one is painting a shield, the objects will first be drawn on it. Meditation should be done before making the shield so one is clear about what symbols are important. Sometimes a shield is made after first going on a Vision Quest or before putting oneself out in the world in a new way. Shields can also be made for each of the four directions. The process of making one's own shield (or shields) enables one to get in touch with the four directions and their corresponding qualities in a very profound way. Begin with any direction that speaks to you. If you are working on issues of trust and faith, reconnecting with your childlike self, start with a south shield. If you are involved in self-healing, start with a west shield. If you are seeking wisdom from ancestors, start with north. And, if you are approaching a turning point in your life for which you need inner vision and new ideas, you might start with east. Wherever you begin, eventually you will be led to the other directions.

Just as our clans, lodges, and covens have medicine bags, so, too, do they have shields. A group shield may contain symbols that are part of the group's medicine, for example, bird or animal parts that empower the group's purpose or express the group's vision. It may embody objects contributed by each member or be painted by one member with the group's input. One of the women's lodges I belong to is called Rainbow Feathers. We have a small shield, drawn by one woman, with many rainbow colored feathers and other objects glued on to give off a sparkling, iridescent effect.

Drums

Drums are the heartbeat of the Earth Mother, and as such, are an integral ingredient in medicine ways. Drums recreate many natural rhythms, including the rhythms of our own breath and heart. They enable us to move into a deeply meditative state where we feel in tune with the cosmos. Drumming is used as a background for chanting, dancing, and for shamanic journeying (a technique of inner traveling to the lower and upper realms to seek out information and vision). Drumming is used in many ceremonies including most Native American and African ones. In major ceremonies such as the Native American Sun Dance and at many pow wows, a large drum is used with four people drumming on it at all times. The drummers can change places, but the new drummer must stand next to the person she is changing with in order to tune into the rhythm so the beat will be uninterrupted. I attended a drumming workshop with Brooke Medicine Eagle one summer where we had a large pow wow drum that was kept going continuously throughout the weekend. People took shifts during the night, sleeping in sleeping bags near the drum so that the heartbeat of the earth was never stopped.

Obtaining a drum is a significant ritual in itself. The hide of the animal used is an important element. One can communicate with the spirit of the animal through the drum so one may have a preference for elk, deer, cow, or goat. The wood chosen for the rim is also important, both for the quality of the sound as well as for the symbolism of the particular tree spirit involved. The harder the wood, the better the sound. Cedar is often used, also birch, redwood, and oak. Many other woods have been used because each native tribe utilized the wood found in its own region. The way the drum is constructed will determine the range of the sound and how it responds to cold, damp, or wet weather (when it tends to get flat) or to hot dry weather (when it gets too tight). In damp weather, a hair dryer, heater, or open fire is used to heat up the drum; in hot dry weather, spraying the drum with water will cool it down.

After you have chosen your drum, it is important to begin a relationship with it. This involves talking to the drum, placing it in a special place in your home, perhaps feeding it cornmeal or tobacco, determining what its function is (Is it a healing drum, a singing drum, a dancing drum, or a drum for special rituals?)

and painting or decorating it with any of your particular totems. Many medicine teachers and tribes don't paint their drums, but they attach certain objects, such as a feather, to it. If you paint a special design on your drum, it is good to use earth colors and keep the painting harmonious with the spirit of the animal whose hide is involved.

At the drumming workshop with Brooke Medicine Eagle, we performed a very beautiful drum naming ceremony. Everyone received some tobacco which had been blessed and each person sprinkled her drum with water while speaking the drum's name and telling what it was here for. Some of the names expressed strong emotions such as "Howling Wolf" or "Dancing Feet." The drums were able to speak out and communicate their deep purpose.

Rattles

If drums are the heartbeat of the Earth Mother, then rattles are her brains. Rattles make a very different sound from drums because they are higher pitched. Rattles are used in many ways in ceremony: at the beginning and end, to call in the four directions, or with the drum to accompany a chant or dance. In Native American church rituals, a small drum and a rattle are passed around the circle to each participant. Each person has the opportunity to drum or rattle and sing a song in turn. Rattles are also used for shamanic journeying; sometimes every person rattles rather than just one person in order to enter into an altered state. I did a journey with rattles once with Norma Cordell, a medicine teacher from Eugene, Oregon. She gave each of us two rattles, one in each hand, and we were never allowed to stop rattling. She talked us through leaving the surface of the earth to enter the lower realm and come back again, all the while continuing to rattle. It was an extremely powerful experience.

Rattles are made from gourds. Gourds grow deep in the earth's soil with tendrils that come out and reach toward the sky. The fruit of the gourd has a hard outer cover that contains many seeds. These seeds are within a watery, pulpy mass until the gourd dries out; then they begin to rattle. It is relatively simple to grow gourds if you have enough space in your garden (like squashes they take a bit of room). There are about thirteen different varieties of gourd seeds; they can be obtained from Native Seeds Search, 2509 N. Campbell

Ave., #325, Tucson, AZ 85719. In their catalogue (available for $1.00), they show pictures of the various types of gourds, so you can decide which shape you want for your rattle.

The symbolism of the gourd and its shape are very important. The gourd represents the earth; its shape resembles the very earliest goddess figures with their full bellies, pregnant with the fertility of the earth. Dolores La Chapelle, in her book, *Sacred Land, Sacred Sex, Rapture of the Deep*, tells us that the gourd is incestuous because pollen from a male flower will fertilize a female flower on the same plant. This explains one of the ancient creation myths. A brother and a sister take refuge in a safe container (a gourd) from a flood. All the other people drown, and when the brother and sister are safe on the land, they ask the animals what to do. The tortoise and the bamboo tell them to marry one another; out of their union a gourd is born. When the woman sows the seeds of the gourd in the ground, these seeds become humans.[6]

After the gourds are dried, they are blessed and then painted and decorated to become rattles. Different tribal cultures use particular symbols on their rattles; for example, Huichol rattles often have a snake on them. It is good to make a rattle with your own symbols and decorations, so that it becomes a tool for empowerment. As with drums, rattles should be named and taken care of. You may have several rattles for different purposes or ceremonies. Commercial rattles such as castanets from Mexico can be repainted and blessed to become your own medicine rattles.

Wands

In the Wiccan tradition, each High Priestess has a wand which she often makes herself. It may be made from a branch of a tree or some other wood. Some wands have crystals on one end. Others have different colored ribbons, herbs, flowers, or feathers attached. Since the wand is used in casting the circle, it should be made into an object of magic and beauty.

Talking Sticks

Most groups that perform rituals and ceremonies have talking sticks. A talking stick or a talking staff is a stick acquired in nature, perhaps part of a branch of a special tree that is native to the area. The branch is a connection to the earth energy, communication with the natural forces that tend to ground mental energy. It is often decorated with feathers or shells and becomes the focal point for the group. By having each person speak only when she is holding the staff, a sense of truth and depth is imparted to the discussion. (The word *truth* comes from the Indo-European root *deru* or *dru* which means "oak" or "tree." A druid is one who sees the tree.[7])

The staff helps us focus our thoughts and also listen to the ideas of others. Listening with the heart is as important as speaking from the heart. Through listening, we hear the deeper meanings behind words. Sometimes when we are all sharing similar ideas, only our words and tones are different.

Preparing and inaugurating the staff is important. The first time the staff is used, all members of the group should bring something they want to tie on to the staff. Often leather pieces are brought or some type of colored wool or twine so that one has something to stroke when the staff is passed; feathers and shells are often tied onto the staff as well. A mixture of herbs such as sage, cedar, tobacco, and cornmeal are often fed to the stick to bless it and connect it with other earth elements.

ENDNOTES

1. Teish, Luisah, *Jambalaya*, Harper & Row, San Francisco, 1985, p. 239.

2. Stein, Diane, *Casting the Circle*, The Crossing Press, Freedom, CA, p. 50.

3. *Ibid.*

4. Teish, p. 240.

5. *Ibid.*, p. 241.

6. La Chapelle, Dolores, *Sacred Land, Sacred Sex, Rapture of the Deep*, p. 96.

7. *Ibid.*, p. 294.

Moon Cycles and Monthly Rituals

The moon has always been the primary symbol for female energy; its cycle around the earth takes approximately twenty-nine days, the same amount of time as the average woman's menstrual cycle. It is often felt that as the pull of the moon affects the waters of the world, so does its motion affect the body of woman. The moon is changeable as it waxes and wanes during the month; at first hidden; later full, round, and swollen. These characteristics of changeability and secrecy are often attributed to women. As a satellite to the earth, the moon is considered the "lesser light," reflecting, but not generating, the light of the sun. So are women often treated as satellites of men.

Originally, the ancients thought that a woman's body and emotions reflected the phases of the moon as it moved from one new moon to the next. The moon's cycle takes about 29-1/4 days. From new moon to full moon the moon waxes or increases in light. This period is considered a good time for seeding new ideas and building form and structure. Under the new moon, when the night remains dark, people tend to work intuitively and instinctually. As the light increases, the growing moon raises consciousness. The full moon marks the time of the greatest light, offering objective awareness. More children are born (brought forth into the light) at the full moon than at any other time. Often it was thought that the influence of the full moon was so powerful that its bright light caused "lunacy" or madness from seeing too clearly. Seeds that were planted at the new moon will blossom or fructify at the full moon—a time when what was created in the dark is brought forth into the light and shared by the outside world.

A woman's blood and hormonal cycle follows the ebb and flow of the moon; from new moon to full moon, estrogen increases leading to ovulation, or maximum fertility, at full moon. From full moon to new moon, the waning half of the cycle, progesterone predominates. Traditionally, women used to start bleeding right before the new moon, in the dark of the moon.

In modern times, women begin their menstruation during different phases of the moon. Their bodies are out of sync with the moon and their spirits have forgotten the meaning of Grandmother Moon. One way to get back in harmony with the moon is by performing ceremonies and rituals at different times during the 29-1/4 day cycle and also by honoring the time of menstruation.

Honoring a Woman's Moon Time

When a woman begins her monthly bleeding, she has a very special vibration. The blood flow is cleansing; as the old uterine lining is sloughed off, one monthly reproductive cycle is ended. At menstruation, women have the chance to rid themselves of all old thoughts, habits, desires, and be receptive to new visions and inspirations for the next cycle. This is the dark moon phase.

If a woman continues her normal routine at menstruation, then she loses a uniquely female opportunity for introspection. She also finds she gets more tired, irritable, and upset because her physical rhythm has slowed down. She needs rest, more time for meditation, and less time doing housework, cooking, working in the outside world, and taking care of children. PMS (premenstrual syndrome) has become such a major health problem because as the hormones change, the level of minerals such as potassium, calcium, and magnesium drop. Women feel these changes in their bodies and their psyches. With the drop in certain minerals and also the B vitamins, such as B-6, women naturally feel more tense and anxious, more sensitive and vulnerable. When they know that they have to continue their daily routine for the five or six days before and during their menstrual period, they experience increased anxiety, accounting for the cramps, headaches, low blood sugar, and other symptoms present before the onset of one's moon time.

PMS symptoms can be controlled by taking extra minerals during the month, especially a potassium-magnesium supplement, and some extra B vitamins. They can also be controlled by drinking herb teas that balance hormones (red raspberry leaf, squawvine, and sarsaparilla root). Sarsaparilla root simmered with licorice root or black cohosh can be drunk a few days before menstruation. The Chinese herb *dong quai* is also excellent to use during the month, a few times a week, preferably simmered as a tea, though it can be obtained in capsules and tablets. Evening primrose oil capsules work well to balance hormones.

One subtle practice that women can do during their moon time to help balance energy was taught to me by my friend, Oh Shinnah. Oh Shinnah said that if you have to go out into the world during your moon time, you may wear a small moonstone in your navel held in place with some surgical tape. The moonstone will balance out your energy and help you feel more grounded when forced to interact with the world.

Simply taking supplements and herbs, while helpful, is not enough. Your cycle has to be honored; time needs to be spent in solitude away from others and away from your daily routine. The best way to do this is to set up a moon lodge or hut, which might be shared by several women, where one can retreat, even if only for a few hours. Some women are able to place a tipi or tent outside on accessible land, but a room in a large house, away from the center of energy, may be used. And, if neither of those places is possible, women can spend time near a personal altar, resting and meditating. A small amount of time used in ritual practice during this cycle is something every woman owes to herself if she wishes to maintain physical and emotional balance.

In a tribal group I belonged to years ago, some families arranged to have the men take over the cooking and child care when the women were in their moon time. Each woman got extra time to rest, meditate, and tune into deeper psychic levels. In return, each woman was easier to be around when she was premenstrual because she knew she would be able to get some time to herself.

Even with the most responsible jobs, a woman can usually take time off in the evenings and mornings, perhaps use her sick leave on occasion, to make some sacred inner space available. Women may also help each other by watching each other's children and doing each other's cooking. Friendships deepen between women when they unite to honor their moon time. One advantage of forming women's lodges or groups is to have a supportive sisterhood which allows each woman some psychic space during the month.

In many Native American tribes and other tribal cultures, there is a separate moon lodge to which all women go. Since most women menstruated at the same time during the dark of the moon, the grandmothers and fathers took care of the children. Food was left outside the lodge several times a day. Women during menstruation were/are considered to hold a certain power and not allowed to mingle with the rest of the tribe. Many tribes have taboos against these women, believing that their power would interfere with the hunt or take away the power of the medicine bundles. This is also why women are not allowed in sweat lodges and must stand outside the circles in other ceremonies when they are in their moon time. We know now that women were also segregated because of fear of the immense power which enabled them to bleed each month and never die—the greatest of all the Mysteries—while a male warrior might succumb quickly after losing so much blood.

There are many rituals and inner processes that we as women can do during our moon time. Most important is to understand what emotions or fears we are letting go of. Did we fear we might be pregnant? What are our desires or disappointments? Did we want to conceive during this last cycle? Calling on the wisdom of the Goddess or our grandmothers and ancestors to help us and guide us through the next cycle may be appropriate. Lighting candles, chanting, praying, dancing—all are useful to ready ourselves for our next cycle or for the new moon. We ask ourselves, "What is it that we might do differently this next cycle?"

Brooke Medicine Eagle has a song that may be used during a woman's moon time:

Blood of Life

I give away this blood of life to all my relations,
And I open my womb to the light.
Give away, give away, give away, give away,
I open my womb to the light.

(Repeat first two lines twice
then repeat third and fourth lines)

(Tape: *A Gift of Song*)

The Fourfold Cycle of the Moon

Before discussing particular moon ceremonies, let's explore further the phases of the moon. I would suggest every woman buy herself a moon calendar or datebook at the beginning of each year. For a woman, using a moon calendar is a sacred and ritualistic act in itself as well as a very practical way to keep track of one's menstrual periods.

The moon's phases can be seen as either four or eight. In a fourfold phase division, the first phase is from new moon to first quarter. During this period energy is initiated, fresh impulses are felt, and forward movement is experienced. This phase corresponds to the direction of east, sunrise, and new beginnings.

From first quarter to full moon, energy builds up, and forms are being perfected. This phase corresponds to south, the fire, the power and strength of summer, and high noon.

In the third phase, from full moon to last quarter, energy is distributed and meaning is injected into the form. We are now in the west, the setting sun, and glean the wisdom inherent in the encroaching darkness.

From last quarter to new moon, forms are broken down and meaning is gathered during the dark of the moon to be released at the next new moon. This phase represents the north, the winter of our lives, a time of wisdom and introspection, a time to commune with all of the dark places within, but also a time when the new year is born.

Our physiology follows these four phases, each phase lasting about seven days. In the first cycle, while estrogen is increasing, we have more energy and tend to be emotionally buoyant; as the full moon nears, our vaginal mucus builds up, sexual drive increases, our nervous system is stimulated, we feel emotionally charged, and tend to sleep less. At full moon, the body releases an egg, which may or may not be fertilized. During the third phase, after the full moon, our estrogen level drops, emotions become more stable, and we have deeper and longer sleep patterns as progesterone predominates. If an egg has been fertilized, the progesterone produces a secretion that nourishes it.

During the fourth phase, after the last quarter moon, if we have not become pregnant, the body releases the uterine lining prepared for the egg. Now we may feel depressed, irritable, anxious, or sad, based on our hormonal levels or perhaps on our wanting to conceive during the last cycle. Anxiety may be present if we are uncertain whether we have conceived and don't want a child at this time. However, when we are following ancient moon rituals and are attuned to our bodies, we know from our dreams when we have conceived. And, we are also able to control when we choose to conceive and bear children through conscious conception.

Eightfold Cycle of the Moon

The four phases of the moon correspond to the four seasons with the equinox and solstice points. The rituals we perform at each phase will also relate to the corresponding equinox or solstice. In between the equinoxes and solstices, however, are the cross-quarter days—those celebrations which were equally important in all earth-centered religions. These eight points correspond also to the Celtic Wheel of the Year and are ritually celebrated in all pagan traditions. The four days are Candlemas or Brigit's Day on February 2, Beltane or May Day on May 1, Lammas on August 1, and All Hallows on October 31.

All earth-based cultures begin their year and their calendar at the Winter Solstice, the time the light begins to increase. It was at this time that the divine son was born, the consort of the moon goddess. In ancient Egypt the archetypal couple was Isis and Osiris; in Sumeria, Inanna and Dmuzzi; in Babylonia, Ishtar and Tammuz. There are many other divine couples in other cultures.

The eight phases of the moon, then correspond in the following way to the eight yearly rituals:

New Moon

- Moon is 0–45 degrees ahead of the sun.
- Moon rises at dawn, sets at sunset.
- Moon is from exact new moon to 3-1/2 days after.
- The seed or project is initiated; an instinctive time, energy is within.
- Winter Solstice, December 21.

Crescent

- Moon is 45–90 degrees ahead of the sun.
- Moon rises mid-morning, sets after sunset.
- Moon is 3-1/2 to 7 days after the new moon.
- The new seed is challenged to move forward; a time of struggle.
- Candlemas, February 2, the beginnings of spring are felt.

First Quarter

- Moon is 90–135 degrees ahead of the sun.
- Moon rises at noon, sets at midnight.
- Moon is from 7 to 10-1/2 days after the new moon.
- The new project takes form; a critical time as it establishes itself in its environment; a time of action.
- Spring Equinox, March 21.

Gibbous

- Moon is 135–180 degrees ahead of the sun.
- Moon rises in mid-afternoon, sets around 3 A.M.
- Moon is between 10-1/2 to 14 days after the new moon.
- A time to analyze the form of the seed or project; a time to perfect.
- Beltane, May 1.

Full Moon

- Moon is 180–225 degrees ahead of the sun.
- Moon rises at sunset, sets at dawn.
- Moon is from 14 to 17-1/2 days after the new moon.
- The illumination and full meaning of the project is revealed.
- Summer Solstice, June 21.

Disseminating

- Moon is 225–270 degrees ahead of the sun.
- Moon rises at mid-evening, sets at mid-morning.
- Moon is 3-1/2 to 7 days after the full moon.
- The meaning of the project or idea is disseminated or shared.
- Lammas, August 1.

Last Quarter

- Moon is 270–315 degrees ahead of the sun.
- Moon rises at midnight and sets at noon.
- Moon is 7 to 10-1/2 days after the full moon.
- The breakdown of form, dissolution.
- Fall Equinox, September 21.

Balsamic (Dark Moon)

- Moon is 315–360 degrees ahead of the sun.
- Moon rises at 3 A.M., sets mid-afternoon.
- Moon is 10-1/2 to 14 days after the full moon.
- The impulse for new forms comes from dreams.
- All Hallows, October 31.

Moon Rituals

At each new moon, every woman should make an altar. On the altar she places symbols of the four directions—a feather or incense for east, candles for south, water for west, and a crystal or cornmeal for north. She may also place a mirror on the altar to see herself as a reflection of the Goddess, a bowl or cauldron in the center as a container for receiving the goddess energy, and the reproduction of a particular goddess figure. It is fitting to place herbs or flowers that are special to the season on the altar. Remember that the new moon is the time to initiate the project that you have been bringing up from your unconscious during the dark moon. If there is an object which will represent the new project or new focus, place it on the altar as well. By using your altar to conduct personal rituals, you can follow the phases of the moon. The arrangement of objects may be changed at each moon phase.

By attuning to the moon, a woman may regulate her bleeding cycle to correspond with the moon's phases. This is better accomplished by going outdoors and performing rituals in the light of the moon or by having the moonlight enter her bedroom so her body is bathed with the light.

Many years ago, Louise Lacey, author of *Lunaception*, worked with twenty-nine women to regulate their cycles. Noting the effect the moon had on the fertility cycle of animals, she perceived that women could regulate their cycles if they left some light on in their bedrooms; this would function like the light of the moon. She had them leave a lamp on during days 14, 15, and 16 of their menstrual cycle. This helped them regulate their ovulation and menstruation.

In order to have your menstrual cycles correspond to those of Grandmother Moon herself, it is best to do moon rituals outdoors, preferably with a group of women or a lodge, since women who spend a lot of time together tend to synchronize their menstrual periods. Objects are placed in the four directions. If you are working within the Wiccan tradition, you would first cast the circle; if you already have a medicine wheel constructed, you would use that as your circle. After each woman is smudged, the four directions (or the six directions including Earth Mother and Sky Father) are called in; then the Goddess is invoked. She may be invoked as the goddess who represents the phase of the moon and the astrological sign in which the lunation is taking place.

For the new moon, Persephone, in her aspect as the virgin daughter, or Artemis (Diana), the virgin goddess of the hunt, may be called on. For the full moon, Aphrodite (Venus), Isis, Ishtar, or Astarte, are sexual goddesses who symbolize the fertility of the full moon. Demeter may also be invoked as she is the Mother and earth goddess, who is symbolic of the full phase, as well as Selene, the Greek moon goddess. At the dark of the moon we have come to the end of the cycle and need to work with the dark aspect of the Goddess. Here, the Goddess is invoked as Hecate, Kali, Medusa, Pele, Sekhmet, or Oya.

New Moon

If one woman is leading the ritual, then she is taking the role of High Priestess. After calling in the directions and the Goddess, she speaks about the significance of this particular new moon in astrological or allegorical terms. Then each woman shares what she desires to manifest during the next cycle. Sometimes a medicine bag is made in which each woman adds a sacred object. This can then be used for healing when any of the women present need it. Sometimes the priestess leads the women through a chakra clearing, bringing down the energy of the moon into each chakra. Later, chants are sung to the moon.

After chanting, the Goddess is thanked, the energies from each direction are thanked, and the ritual is ended. Sharing of other chants and special moon foods are pleasant ways to end the ceremony.

Full Moon

At full moon we celebrate fulfillment, fertility, and the bearing of fruit from our projects. We call in the directions with our drums and rattles in a spirit of celebration. We call in the Goddess in her full sexuality; we call in the Mother in her abundant nurturing aspect. Then, looking up to the moon, if she is visible in the sky, (and, if not, visualizing her there) we draw down the moon into our bodies. Drawing down the moon is an old pagan ritual done by raising ones eyes up to the moon and by lifting one's arms overhead so that they create a chalice of one's body to receive the moon's energy. With this moon manna coursing through her body, each woman can invoke the energies she wants on the full moon, ask for her special prayers to be answered by the moon mother, and may make any affirmations important to her.

After each woman has gone through this ritual, the group may share their feelings, prayers, chants to Grandmother Moon, and any other singing, drumming, and dancing that is inspired by the ritual. Dancing outdoors under the full moon is an ecstatic experience; if the weather is warm, dancing naked allows one to experience the moon's juice flowing through each of the body's centers. Dancing together allows us to become one with the moon goddess and with women everywhere.

Here is a chant to honor Grandmother Moon from the Bear tribe:

> Into the silence of the night,
> Into the silence of the moon,
> I am making my dreams come true.
> Into the silence of the night,
> Into the silence of the moon,
> I am making my being come true.

> (Tape: *Medicine Wheel Chants*,
> Bear Tribe Medicine Society,
> P.O.Box 9167, Spokane, WA 99209)

Mother Moon

> In thy power, Mother moon,
> I put my faith again.

> (Repeat)[1]

Dark Moon

The dark of the moon is the time of menstruation and, conversely, also signifies menopause; it is the time of the Goddess Hecate, the Crone, and mother of the dark moon. In the dark of the moon we allow our seeds and our projects to disintegrate, to go back into the earth, to be cleansed and reborn into the new cycle approaching. Our souls go underground, into the depths of the earth, to look deeply and let go of old habits or patterns we wish to shed. To experience our blood when we are menstruating is to experience what that blood flowing out of our bodies cleanses from our souls. We experience the depth and darkness of our sensuality just as at full moon we experienced this sensuality in the light. We feel what it is to be a woman, to hold the mystery of life and death, to bleed every month, to work our magic.

For dark moon ceremonies, we often choose black candles for the altar or red ones to symbolize blood. We choose owl wings, for owls are the creatures of the night or sometimes the skulls of animals to represent death. We place representations of the dark goddesses—Kali, Medusa, Pele, Hecate, Oya, Lilith—on our altars, and it is these goddesses that we invoke in our rituals.

As we stand in the darkness in our circle, we feel the absence of the Moon Mother, the sadness of her departure underground. We speak to her and banish to her everything we want to shed from our lives now. And as we do this, we feel her within us; we feel her seeds stirring for the new cycle; we feel ourselves cleansed and made whole from the darkness. And then we dance, drum, and chant to allow ourselves to celebrate this release from the old—the completion and the rebirth. Our dancing may be wild and ecstatic as we call on the Dark Mother; our sounds may be shrill and off-key, and our blood may stain the ground. We grieve for and celebrate all who have passed to another realm, all who are passing, all who are moving through the dark underground to heal themselves.

Here is an invocation to Kali that we may use at this time:

Invocation to Kali

Kali, Oh Kali Ma,
Dark Mother and Protector,
You who go into the battlefields
    of humanity,
Devouring the demons,
Piercing through our illusions,
Beautiful, destroying Mother.

Kali, Oh Kali Ma,
Dark Mother and Protector,
You who dance in ecstasy
    in the graveyards,
with skulls adorning your breast,
and peacock feathers,
Beautiful, destroying Mother.

Kali, Oh Kali Ma,
Dark Mother and Protector,
Purify us with your fire,
your wrath, and your anger,
so that we may be free
of greed, selfishness, and
    delusion.
Beautiful, destroying Mother.

New Moon and Full Moon Ceremonies in the Yearly Cycle

There are almost thirteen moon cycles in a solar year. Some years have thirteen new moons and other have thirteen full moons. When a month has two full moons, it is often called a blue moon month (thus, the expression, "once in a blue moon").

Each new moon and each full moon occurs in a different astrological sign and has a different symbolic meaning. At new moon, the sun and the moon are together and in the same sign, but the moon itself is hidden from view so the solar emphasis is stronger. At full moon, the sun and the moon are exactly opposite each other and in opposite signs. Here the moon's energy beams directly down on the earth; however, the solar energy of the opposite sign is also at work. The signs with their opposites are: Capricorn/Cancer, Aquarius/Leo, Pisces/Virgo, Aries/Libra, Taurus/Scorpio, and Gemini/Sagittarius. Starting with the Winter Solstice, we will travel through the new and full moons in the yearly cycle.

New Moon in Capricorn

The first new moon of the cycle may happen close to the Winter Solstice. (The Druidic calendar starts with the Winter Solstice and has thirteen months of twenty-eight days each, with one day left over. The leftover day is considered the most sacred day of the year.[2]) The new moon in Capricorn is symbolic of strong new beginnings, both for this moon cycle and for the entire year. It is the beginning of light returning as the sun begins its yearly ascent and days begin to get longer. During Capricorn, the horned or goat god is reborn to seed the spring and die with the waning of the year. Capricorn is a time for setting down foundations and plans for the year ahead, as Capricorn is an earth sign representing structure and order. It is a time for setting boundaries in our lives and in our relationships, boundaries that we want to maintain in the next cycle and year. It is also a time for making both short- and long-term plans.

Earth colored candles—oranges, browns, yellows—may be placed on our altar. Stones such as onyx and jet which are black and ruled by the planet Saturn (ruler of Capricorn) may also be used. Capricorn is symbolized by the sure-footed goat who climbs slowly to the top of the mountain. There is steadfastness and perseverance in his climb. For this lunation, we might attempt a hike, climbing up a mountain or hill top where we can hold our ritual.

Since Capricorn is an earth sign, pictures and invocations of earth goddesses would be appropriate. Sharing stories of Gaia, the most ancient Earth Mother, or of Demeter could be a part of the ceremony. Chants to the Earth Mother may also be included.

Here is a chant I like for the Earth Mother:

The Earth Is Our Mother
(*adaptation of a Hopi chant*)

The Earth is our Mother,
We must take care of her.
The Earth is our Mother,
We must take care of her.
Hey yunga ho yunga hey yung yung
Hey yunga ho yunga hey yung yung
Her sacred ground we walk upon
With every step we take.
Her sacred ground we walk upon
With every step we take.
Hey yunga ho yunga hey yung yung
The Mother gives her life to us
With every seed we plant.

(Repeat two lines)
Hey yunga ho yunga hey yung yung
Hey yunga ho yunga hey yung yung

The air we breathe is freedom
With every breath we take.

(Repeat two lines)
Hey yunga ho yunga hey yung yung
Hey yunga ho yunga hey yung yung[3]

(Tape: *The Giveaway*,
Ojai Foundation,
P.O. Box 5037, Ojai, CA 93023)

Full Moon in Cancer (*Sun in Capricorn*)

On the first full moon of the year, we honor the Mother and the children. Cancer is a sign of nurture, a water sign; its symbol is the breasts. Placing fertile pregnant goddesses on our altar will help us focus on maternal qualities. We can begin our ceremony by talking about what we need to nurture in ourselves and others, especially during the dark winter months. Then we can concentrate on the children of the planet, particularly in those areas where children are malnourished,

poor, or dying of disease. Since we live in a country that does not respect children, we can pay special attention to the many children in our society who receive inadequate care or are abused. We can send healing thoughts to these children and children everywhere. Because the moon rules Cancer, this is a superb time to do a full moon ceremony and call in all the moon goddesses. Here is a good water song for the Cancer full moon.

The River
The river she is flowing,
Flowing and growing,
The river she is flowing,
Down to the sea.
Mother, carry me,
A child I will always be
Mother, carry me,
Down to the sea.[4]

(Tape: *Songs to the Goddess*,
Sonoma County Birth Network,
P.O. Box 1005, Occidental, CA 95465)

New Moon in Aquarius

The new moon in Aquarius occurs between January 21 and February 21, a time of year when we are usually indoors by a warm fire. Aquarius is a sign of humanitarian projects; it speaks of freedom and individuality. To connect with this energy in ourselves, we might call the goddess Athena into our ceremonial circle. Athena is the Greek goddess of wisdom; she was born fullgrown from the head of Zeus and has less connection with the mothering, feminine energy of some of the other goddesses. She represents the Aquarian prototype, often cold and detached, yet having some of the most "far out" ideas.

Blue corn seeds are good on the altar at this time because blue is the color related to Aquarius. Crystals and gems such as aquamarine, lapis lazuli, sapphire, and azurite would also be appropriate as well as some blue candles. This is a time when we can seed ideas for projects that will help humanity and commit ourselves to working on these projects for the next cycle.

Since many people feel we are entering the Aquarian Age, it might be helpful to discuss in the circle what the Aquarian Age signifies to us. As the talking stick is passed around, we can consider how we can work together as a community and yet not lose our individual freedoms.

Full Moon in Leo (*Sun in Aquarius*)

If, at the new moon in Aquarius we started on projects to benefit humanity, they may have reached a peak point now where we can share them with others, organize them, receive criticism from the outside world, and express them in a creative form. Leo has much creative energy. Leo also rules the heart, so if we feel our emotional energy is blocked, this lunation is a good time to look within our hearts and let our emotions surface and burst forth.

At this cold time of the year, it is especially important to feel each other's love and warmth as we circle around the fire, chanting, dancing, calling in our full moon goddesses—Aphrodite, Astarte, Selene. We draw down the moon and feelings of love and warmth for all humanity into our hearts as we dance for freedom and chant the following:

I Will Burn with the Fire of Freedom (*Starhawk*)
Oh, I will burn with the fire of Freedom,
Truth is the Fire that will burn our chains,
I will stop the Fires of destruction,
Healing is the Fire burning through my veins.[5]

(Tape: *Chants-Ritual Music*,
Reclaiming Collective)

New Moon in Pisces

Invocation to Kwan Yin
Oh, Kwan Yin, most merciful Mother,
Merciful and loving,
Compassionate, beautiful.
We call upon you now,
Come to us in our time of need.
Soothe us, Holy Mother,
Embrace us with your love,
Your compassion, your beauty.
So that we might become whole,
And walk a gentle path
On this Earth.

The new moon in Pisces occurs between February 21 and March 21, shortly before Spring Equinox. Pisces is the twelfth sign of the zodiac and relates to spiritual initiation and immersion, including development of psychic and healing abilities. In Pisces we develop compassion for ourselves and others.

Purple candles and crystals such as amethyst and flourite may be used to decorate the altar. (Purple is the color of the seventh ray which emanates through the crown chakra.) Purplish herbs such as lavender may be put on the altar as well as feathers from birds, so we can give thanks to them for their gifts. For the Pisces moon, we call in Kwan Yin (the Chinese goddess of compassion). *Ku'an* means "earth" and *Yin* means "woman" so Kwan Yin is another earth woman or nature goddess. During the ritual, we can share how to be more compassionate and less judgmental in thought and action, taking care to demonstrate these qualities during the ceremony. What seed do we plant within ourselves to bring about this compassion? Perhaps the group will decide to contribute time or energy to a project involved with healing others. Perhaps individuals will decide to use meditation or art work to bring healing to themselves. The Pisces energy is undifferentiated; it is the "oceanic feeling" by which we connect with all other living beings.

Here is a song for Kwan Yin that I learned years ago from the Sufis:

Kwan Yin, Bo Sa,
Kwan Yin, Bo Sa,
Kwan Yin, Bo Sa,
Kwan Yin, Bo.

Full Moon in Virgo (*Sun in Pisces*)

The Virgo full moon also takes place between February 21 and March 21. Decorate the altar with earth colors and earth-colored gems such as agates and tiger's eye. Call in the spirits of the flowers and plants now resting underground, but about to burst forth in spring. At the new moon we experienced becoming more compassionate; now we can share with one another how these sympathetic feelings have changed us. Since Virgo is a sign of service, we also share our ideas on healing and working for others. Now is a time to fill ourselves up with the gentleness of the moon because under Virgo we can sometimes be critical and too analytical.

As we draw down the moon into our beings, we visualize the gentleness of the moon goddesses—Diana/Artemis in the forest with the animals, or Kwan Yin nurturing all the creatures of the earth.

And we sing:

I will be gentle with myself,
I will love myself,
I am a child of the universe,
We are one together.

(Tape: *The Giveaway*,
Ojai Foundation)

New Moon in Aries

Invocation to Pele

Oh, Pele,
Volcano Goddess of Hawaii,
Queen of the islands,
We call upon you.
We give you our rage,
Our lust, and our anger.
That you may cleanse us
With your fiery lava,
That you may empower us
With your mighty flow,
That you may bless us,
With your strange beauty.

The new moon in Aries occurs between March 21 and April 21; it is a time of new beginnings and initiations. Aries is a fire sign, symbolized by the ram, who pushes his way through obstacles and is not always aware of his fellow animals. Fire is a primeval force and many cultures had fire goddesses—the Japanese goddess Fuji (whose name was given to Mt. Fujiyama), the Egyptian goddess Sekhmet, the Hawaiian Pele, the Aztec Cihuacoatl, and the Celtic Brigit.

This lunation might be an appropriate time to do a fire ritual, celebrating the power of fire and calling in the fire goddesses. Fire power makes itself felt in our lives when volcanos erupt, particularly on the big island of Hawaii when Mount Kilauea spews forth, usually causing a lot of destruction. The Hawaiians sacrifice to Pele so that she will not become angry with them and vent her wrath.

Our altar might be decorated with fiery red candles, red stones such as carnelian, ruby, garnet, and blood-stone. Spring herbs and flowers might also be used. The energy of spring is a bursting forth, so let's think about how we use our aggressive energy. Do we use it to accomplish our objectives and assert ourselves powerfully, or do we merely become angry when we are frustrated and then are unable to change the situation?

Full Moon in Libra (*Sun in Aries*)

This full moon also occurs between March 21 and April 21. It is the lunation closest to Easter and marks the Jewish Passover festival. The resurrection of the Christ spirit, the spirit of Love, derives from the Eostara celebration in the Goddess religions. Eostara was the German goddess of re-birth; all the fertility symbols (Easter eggs and bunnies) were associated with her. Easter is a celebration of the renewal of the earth's fertility. Passover marks the Jews' release from bondage when they crossed through the Red Sea and were delivered from the Egyptians. So at this time, we might ask, what parts of ourselves need to be renewed, what parts are still in bondage?

Libra is a sign of relationships, while Aries rules the self, the "I am." Are we walking in balance in our relationships? Are we spending enough time with ourselves? Here is a good chant to help focus on balance.

Give Thanks to the Mother Gaia

Give thanks to the Mother Gaia,
Give thanks to the Father Sun,
Give thanks to the beautiful garden,
Where the Mother and Father are one.

Give thanks, give thanks,
For you we do give thanks.
Give thanks, give thanks,
For you we do give thanks.[6]

(Tape: *Songs to the Goddess*,
Sonoma County Birth Network)

New Moon in Taurus

Invocation to Aphrodite

Golden haired Aphrodite,
Aphrodite with your golden hair,
Arising from the sea,
Surrounded by white foam,
Being birthed by the waters.

Aphrodite, bless us
With your beauty,
With your love,
With your fertile, pregnant being,
That we may heal the Earth,
And help her to bear fruit.

The new moon in Taurus takes place between April 21 and May 21. The fullness of spring is a time when seeds begin to sprout and the reproduction of the Earth Mother is very strong. The bull was venerated in many ancient earth religions; in the Bronze Age in Crete the bull was especially significant. The myth of the Minotaur, a creature half bull and half human who lived in an elaborate labyrinth underneath the palace at Knossus, was a powerful one. The Minotaur (minos = man) was also another symbol for King Minos, the bull/man who was chosen to be priest king for a cycle of eight to nine years. When the next cycle came around, he had to undergo a religious ordeal supervised by priestesses to see whether he was ready to reassume his priestly functions.[7] When he was in the role of administering justice, he wore women's clothes.

The word *taurus* derives from the Greek *tau*. The *tau*, like our letter "T," originated as a pictogram for sexual intercourse, the short bar symbolizing the vulva and the long bar, the penis.[8]

At this time, we decorate our altar with spring herbs and flowers; green stones of malachite, emerald, aventurine, or chrysolite; and green candles. It is a time to be thankful for the creations of the Earth Mother as we plant our own seeds for this lunar cycle and for the coming year; this is a time of great fertility. We invoke all the fertility goddesses—Aphrodite, Venus, Ishtar, Astarte, Isis.

Full Moon in Scorpio (*Sun in Taurus*)

Invocation to Hecate
O Hecate, Queen of the dark night,
You who stand alone at the crossroads,
With owl wings on your shoulders,
Waiting for lost travelers,
Seeking their destinies.

O Hecate, Lady of the dark moon,
It was you who heard Persephone's cries,
When she was taken to the Underworld,
You who create magic,
For those making pilgrimages
To caves and tombs, the unseen dark places.

O Hecate, Queen of the Witches,
Magical moon Mother,
Crone Goddess of the dark moon,
We seek your wisdom.

This important full moon, known as the Wesak full moon, the Buddha's birthday, occurs between April 21 and May 21. While Taurus is an earth sign of fertility, Scorpio is a water sign symbolizing transformation,

death, and re-birth. The awakening of the kundalini energy that lies dormant at the seat of our spine is a Scorpionic experience. So, too, is our body's process of reproduction and excretion.

At this full moon, we are ready to shed whatever it is that is holding us back, whatever is not needed any more in our lives. As we shed our old skins, we give birth to new ones.

With black as the color of Scorpio, we use black candles, and crystals such as smoky quartz, obsidian, and jet. We may also use pictures of the dark goddesses—Hecate, Kali, Ereshkigal, Medusa, Lilith, Pele, and Sekhmet. We call in the Dark Mother, asking that she help us let go of our old patterns of bondage and sacrifice to her so that we might be reborn. Here is a wonderful song to sing at this full moon:

Wild Woman
I am a wild woman.
I am a wild woman.
I live in the sands and I walk in the sun,
I am a wild woman.
I am a wild woman.
I sleep on the earth and I dance in the trees,
I live in the sands and I fly on the breeze,
I walk in the sun and I drink with the bees,
I sing with the rocks and I do as I please.
I am a wild woman.
I am a wild woman.

(Tape: *Inner Voice, Songs of the Spirit*)

New Moon in Gemini

The new moon in Gemini takes place between May 21 and June 21, the time of the year preceding Summer Solstice. Gemini is a mutable air sign; just as the summer winds scatter the seeds about, so too, can this be a time of scattered energies. It is also a time for good communication and many new projects.

Since Gemini is the sign of the twins, it symbolizes polarity, yin and yang, feminine and masculine. How can we bring both of these into balance in our own nature and in society?

At this time we might decorate the altar with yellow candles, with special herbs such as lavender (relaxing to the nervous system) and with gems such as agates, tiger's eye, and cat's eye that help to see clearly. We might invoke some of the partner goddesses and gods such as Artemis and Apollo, Isis and Osiris, or Hera and Zeus.

Here is a good chant for Gemini lunations:

Spirit of the Wind

Spirit of the wind, carry me
Spirit of the wind, carry me home,
Spirit of the wind, carry me home to myself.

Spirit of the ocean,
Depths of emotion,
Spirit of the sea,
Set my soul free. (Repeat Spirit of the wind.)

Spirit of the storm,
Help me be reborn,
Spirit of the rain,
Wash away my pain. (Repeat Spirit of the wind.)

Spirit of the sun,
Warm light healing me,
Spirit of the sky,
Spread my wings and fly. (Repeat Spirit of the
   wind.)

Spirit of the river,
Blessed forgiver,
Spirit of the shore,
Show me more and more. (Repeat Spirit of the
   wind.)

Spirit of the earth,
Help me at my birth,
Spirit of the land,
Hold me in your hand. (Repeat Spirit of the
   wind.)[9]

(Tape: *A Gift of Song,*
Brooke Medicine Eagle)

Full Moon in Sagittarius (*Sun in Gemini*)

Invocation to Artemis

Oh, Artemis, mighty huntress,
Queen of the night sky,
Sending down arrows of light.

Oh, Artemis, Bear mother,
Protectress and nurturer,
Give us your strength, wisdom, and valor
So we may send our arrows of truth
Into the heavens.

The full moon in Sagittarius takes place between May 21 and June 21. Rituals may be combined with the Summer Solstice. Sometimes at this lunation we have a tendency to do and plan too many projects, as the Gemini/Sagittarius axis is one of communication, expansion, short and long journeys, philosophy and metaphysics.

The symbol of Sagittarius is the archer with a bow and arrow, shooting wisdom down from the sky. Artemis or Diana is the goddess of the hunt, who stands poised with her bow and arrow. Artemis was the queen of the Amazons, strong women who were at one with the animals and performed many valorous deeds—they even cut off one breast in order to perfect their archery. Diana was the Roman moon goddess and huntress who sent beams from her arrows down from the night sky. We can invoke Artemis at this time, calling her in with the nymphs who followed her throughout the forest. On our altar we can place a bow and arrow, or a picture of Artemis. We can also place pictures of the bear, the animal ally of Artemis. We might call in the attributes of strength and valor that we desire and the energy of the bear for protection and nurturance.

New Moon in Cancer

The new moon in Cancer takes place between June 21 and July 21. The summer has begun, with long hot days and short nights. Cancer is a water sign of nurturing and motherhood; its symbol is a woman's breasts. Cancer is ruled by the moon.

On our altars we may place silver candles, gems such as moonstones, pearls, and opals, and pictures of the moon goddesses—Selene, Isis, Ishtar, Diana, or Ix Chel (Mayan moon goddess). Goddess fertility figures and representations of the Mother from all cultures would be appropriate.

This is a time to seed ideas and projects for the summer months. It is also a time to respect and honor children and mothers. What can we do now to help the children, especially those who are hungry, homeless, and in need of healing?

As we do our ceremony, we might remember the ancient mystery of the moon. It was she who lit up the sky and guided us at night. Many tribal cultures used mind-altering substances such as mushrooms, the peyote cactus, or pulque, (a wine obtained by the

Mexican Indians from the maguey plant). The ancient Hindus drank soma, the wine from the ancient moon tree. These mind-altering substances were related to the moon as they were utilized to bring about higher psychic states of consciousness.

Full Moon in Capricorn (*Sun in Cancer*)

The full moon in Capricorn occurs before July 21. The Cancer/Capricorn polarity relates to issues of security and structure. What needs building at this time? Is there a balance between one's home and work? Have we been able to put our dreams and plans into concrete form?

Our altar may reflect the earth energies of Capricorn with yellows, oranges, browns. Onyx and certain agates may be used. Demeter, Gaia, and other earth goddesses may be exhibited as well as any representations of the horned god, since Capricorn is the sign of the goat (its symbol is the goat combined with the fishes). The goat's horns suggest the crescents of the moon, while the goat itself symbolizes the moon's priestesses who practiced medicine. The fish represents the moon goddess as ruler of the waters and is often depicted as a mermaid.[10]

Now is an important time to bring in Mother energy because the sun is in Cancer. Here is a good song to use, reflecting both the earthy image of Capricorn and the motherly one of Cancer:

Mother I Feel You Under My Feet

Mother I feel you under my feet,
Mother I hear your heart beat.
Hey ya, hey ya, hey ya, hey ya, hey ya, Ho.

Mother I hear you in the river's song,
Eternal waters flowing on and on.
Hey ya, hey ya, hey ya, hey ya, hey ya, Ho.

Mother I see you when the eagle flies,
flight of the spirit going to take us higher.
Hey ya, hey ya, hey ya, hey ya, hey ya, Ho.

(Tape: *A Gift of Song*,
Brooke Medicine Eagle)

New Moon in Leo

Invocation to Sekhmet

Oh, Sekhmet,
Lady of the blazing flame,
Lion headed goddess,

You who dwell in the deserts,
You who send the winds
To heal us and destroy us.

Oh, Sekhmet,
Mother of the dead,
Lady of the waters of life,
You whose courage and power,
Dwells within each of us.

We implore you, Sekhmet,
Be with us now,
Show us the way,
Of your passion,
And your lion's heart.

The time of this lunation is between July 21 and August 21, often the hottest time of the summer when the sun is dazzling and brilliant. Leo is ruled by the sun; the lion who symbolizes Leo is fiery and courageous, the king of the beasts. Leo rules the heart and creative energy. Now is the time to seed projects of a creative nature and to share how we can open our hearts to the creative energies of the universe.

The lion was important in the Goddess religions as a companion to the Goddess. The Egyptian sphinx had a lion's body and a woman's head, whereas the goddess Sekhmet had the head of a lion and a woman's body. Both showed the union of the sun and moon, with the moon representing the goddess. In other cultures the lion was also present with the goddess. In Sparta, the goddess stands on a lion, while in Crete she is shown playing with lions or standing on a mountain top flanked by them.[11] In Phoenicia and Mycenae, the goddess is presented in abstract form as the moon tree or moonstone, with lions standing guard on either side of her.[12] The goddesses Ishtar from Babylonia and Atargatis from Asia Minor are shown astride lions; in Tibet, Tara rides a lion and holds the sun in her hand.[13] The symbolism of the goddess in connection with the lion shows the merging of one's animal and spiritual nature, with the goddess (or spirit) naturally assuming ascendancy over the animal.

Our altars can be decorated with the colors of the sun, golden yellows and oranges. Stones such as citrine, topaz, and amber can be placed around the altar with small figurines of the lion-headed goddesses. We feel the sun's energy enter our solar plexus and invoke the goddess Sekhmet. Sekhmet is a protectress of the divine order; she protects the gods when they are attacked. Her methods of destruction include fire, pestilence, and drought. Sekhmet's primary dwelling place was in the desert where she roamed in her full lioness body. Although she sent hot winds carrying disease to her enemies, she was also the goddess of healing. She was known as the goddess of fertility and the one who controls the waters of life.[14] She had the capacity to destroy souls so that they had no afterlife or reincarnation; yet she also protected the dead in the underworld.

Full Moon in Aquarius (*Sun in Leo*)

This lunation occurs between July 21 and August 21, a very hot time of the year in the Northern Hemisphere. This is a time when Native Americans often perform Sun Dance rituals. The Sun Dance is a dance that is done to honor fire, to sacrifice to the power of the sun, to bring the light of the sun into one's inner being, to *illuminate* one's self.

The sign Aquarius is a sign of humanity and humanitarianism; its symbol is the water-bearer who pours the waters of life over us. Water is a symbol of the feminine nurturing energy; Aquarius emphasizes group consciousness rather than individual concerns.

At this time we can decorate our altars with blue candles and blue stones such as sapphire, lapis lazuli, and aquamarine. Blue is a cooling color, working not only to cool us down in the heat, but to "cool out" the Uranian vibrations emanating from the Aquarian lunation. (Aquarius is ruled by the planet Uranus, signifying freedom, rebelliousness, and change.) We might share what we can do at this time to deepen our own commitments to humanity and to participate in humanitarian causes.

Here is a good song for this lunation:

If Every Woman in the World

If every woman in the world had her mind set on freedom,
If every woman in the world dreamed a sweet dream of peace.
If every woman in every nation, young and old, each generation,
Would join hands in the name of love, there would be no more war.
If every man in the world . . . .
If every child in the world . . . .
If every mother in the world . . . .
If every father in the world . . . .

New Moon in Virgo

Invocation to Demeter

Oh Demeter,
Goddess of the golden grain,
Of the golden grain and harvest,
Be with us, Earth Mother,
Heal us and heal our children.

Oh Demeter,
You who have grieved for your daughter
    Persephone,
Spent your time searching the underworld,
You who have returned to us in your glory,
Bless our land and make it fertile.

Oh Demeter,
Sacred Mother,
Blessed sister,
Fruitful earth,
We invoke you now.

The sun enters the sign Virgo about August 21 in late summer. Days have begun to grow shorter, and the feeling of fall is in the air. We know the harvest is not far off as we celebrate this new moon.

The symbol of Virgo is the maiden with a sheath of wheat, representing the Great Goddess as Earth Mother; as Goddess of the Grain; as the Roman Ceres (from which we get the word *cereal*); as the Greek Demeter; as the Egyptian Isis-Hathor; as Chicomecoatl, the Aztec Corn Mother; as the Rice Mother in Asia; and as the Native American Three Sisters (maize, beans, and squash).

There were many ceremonies done at this time of year to honor the corn. In ancient Mexico in a temple to the Mother Chicomecoatl, three young girls were chosen to be corn maidens for the year. The youngest had her hair cropped short to show the young sprouts; the second had her hair falling upon her shoulders to represent the corn half grown; and the oldest of the three had her waist-long hair tied into a braided bun to symbolize the full grown crops. They walked to the temple three times: first to lay the baby sprouts of corn at the feet of Chicomecoatl, second when the maize had grown half-way, and the third time when the corn was high in the fields. At this time seven ears were wrapped in red tissue and carried on their backs.[15]

The Greater Eleusinian Mysteries were also held between September 13 to 22 for the goddess Demeter in Greece. Initiates fasted and performed certain rites in order to experience their own death. The nine days were symbolic of Demeter's nine-month search for her daughter Persephone in the underworld. When Demeter's daughter was abducted to the underworld by Hades, she caused all the crops to dry up and everything on earth to wither and die. The ceremonies to Demeter every year—the Lesser Mysteries in the spring and the Greater Mysteries in the fall—were related to the fertility of the earth as well as to the process of individual death and transformation.

The altar may be decorated with earth colors, yellows, oranges, and browns. Tiger's eye, cat's eye, and earthy colored crystals may be placed around pictures and replicas of the earth goddesses. Colored corn and squash may also adorn the altar as well as seeds from different kinds of corn—yellow, blue, and red. Prayers for the earth's fertility may be shared and gifts given to the Earth Mother. The goddess Demeter may be invoked and brought into the circle. Here is a good chant for this lunation:

> She's been waiting, waiting, she's been waiting so long,
> She's been waiting for her children to remember to return.
> Blessed be and blessed are the lovers of the lady,
> Blessed be and blessed are the mother, maid, and crone.
> Blessed be and blessed are the ones who dance together,
> Blessed be and blessed are the ones who dance alone.[16]

> (Tape: *Songs to the Goddess*,
> Sonoma County Birth Network)

Full Moon in Pisces (*Sun in Virgo*)

Between August 21 and September 21 each year is the harvest moon celebration. This is a time of fullness and celebration of the earth's bounty. On the altar may be placed some of the harvest—fruits, vegetables, herbs, corn.

Pisces symbolizes spiritual fulfillment, so the celebration is not only for the material abundance of the harvest but also for one's inner harvest. The higher attributes of Pisces are compassion and forgiveness while those of Virgo (the sign where the sun is) are service and discrimination.

The symbol of Pisces is the two fishes, one swimming upstream, the other downstream. Fish symbolize fertility, the fertility of the waters and the fertility of the Goddess at this time of year. The two fish seem to indicate that the polarity of the cycle, the death and rebirth aspects, are intertwined, just as in autumn, we experience the fertility of the earth's harvest as she begins her death.

The goddess Kwan Yin may be called in to symbolize the spirit of compassion and gentleness. (See new moon in Pisces for the Invocation to Kwan Yin.) We might discuss the difference between service and sacrifice. Martyrdom is a negative manifestation of Pisces. Where are our boundaries? At what point do we sacrifice ourselves and give too much?

Part of the energy of Pisces and its ruling planet Neptune is poetry and music. This is a good lunation in which to share our poems and songs and also to do some dancing to celebrate the earth's harvest. (Pisces rules the feet.) Here is a good chant for the full moon in Pisces:

> Humble yourself inside of your mother (father) (children)
> You've got to ask her what she knows and
> Humble yourself inside of your mother,
> You've got to know what she knows and
> We shall lift each other up, higher and higher,
> We shall lift each other up, higher and higher,
> We shall lift each other up, higher and higher,
> We shall lift each other up.[17]

> (Tape: *Songs to the Goddess*,
> Sonoma County Birth Network)

New Moon in Libra

Invocation to Athena
Athena, Lady of Wisdom,
With your aegis and goat skin,
With serpents entwined on your arms,
Athena, Lady of Battle,
With your shield and spear,
Your helmeted head,
You who have fought with many,
To bring peace and justice.
You who have woven many tapestries,
To bring art and beauty,
Athena, we invoke you,
Ancient weaver,
Holy one of Athens,
Proud Goddess,
Be with us.

After the Fall Equinox, between September 21 and October 21 we experience the Libran new moon. Libra is a sign of balance, of partnership; its symbol is the scales of justice.

We can use this lunation to see how balanced we are in our relationships (the Aries\Libra polarity) and ask ourselves how much time do we spend alone and how much in relationship? This is a good time to think about community or public service work, as Libran energy can be used to get outside of oneself and into the life of the greater society around one. Libra (as well as Taurus) is ruled by the planet Venus so it is an artistic sign; the balance we perceive in paintings, musical compositions, and poetry is a Libran function. In Libra we think of Venus not as the sensuous and earthy goddess of early spring, but as the goddess who exemplifies the peace and harmony that comes from working together with others and promoting social causes that bring justice to humanity.

To prepare for our ritual, we might decorate the altar with fall flowers, with green candles to symbolize Venus and with malachite, chrysoprase, aventurine, or aquamarine. Then we might invoke the goddess Athena. Athena was known for her wisdom and for her intellect. The oak tree and the olive branch were sacred to Athena. So, while she wore a helmet and carried a shield and spear, she was still associated with peace.

Full Moon in Aries (*Sun in Libra*)

This full moon occurs right around the Fall Equinox, a time when we are preparing for the winter months ahead. Aries is a fire sign symbolized by the ram and ruled by Mars, the god of war. The ram in ancient cultures was always a powerful symbol of masculine energy, so now is a good time to get in touch with aggression and passion. How much do we express and how much do we hold back? How can we be assertive and sensitive at the same time? Or metaphorically, how do we unite the aggressive Aries with the balance of Libra?

The Aries lunation gives us another opportunity to work with ourselves and our relationships. How much time do we need to spend alone and feel fulfilled within ourselves? How much time do we need to put into our relationships?

For our ceremony, we may decorate the altar with red candles, stones such as bloodstone, garnet, and carnelian; and pictures of the fire goddesses as Pele,

Sekhmet, Fuji, and Cihuacoatl. We may then invoke any of these goddesses as we share our fire, anger, and wrath.

New Moon in Scorpio

Invocation to Ix Chel, Great Eagle Woman
Oh Great Eagle Woman,
Moon Mother,
Lighting the way,
Bringing vision,
Soaring over us
With great wings.

Oh Great Eagle Woman,
You bring death and destruction,
You bring birth and creation,
Wisdom woman flying high,
We call on you
To guide us now.

The new moon in Scorpio occurs between October 21 and November 21. The approach of winter forces us to retreat indoors and spend more time alone. All Hallows Eve, the end of the old year in the earth-centered religions, occurs during this period. It is a time when the vegetation dies and souls return from other realms.

Scorpio has many symbols—the scorpion that stings, the eagle that soars over all, the snake that sheds its skin, and the dove of peace. Scorpio is a sign of transformation and rebirth; it reaches to the lowest depths in the bowels of the earth and to the greatest heights in the wings of the eagle. Ix Chel, the Mayan moon goddess, was crowned with the feathers of the Eagle; eagle feathers were woven into her throne. Ix Chel was known as Eagle Woman and eagles were her messengers.[18]

Many goddesses in various cultures were depicted with snakes. The great goddess of Crete was pictured with snakes encircling her arms. The Greek Medusa, one of the dark goddesses, was the only mortal member of the three Gorgons. Her gaze turned men to stone. Her hair was transformed to hissing serpents by Athena because Medusa claimed equal beauty with hers. Perseus killed Medusa, with the help of Athena, by not looking directly at her awful countenance but watching her reflection in his shield while he cut off her head. Her head was then placed on Athena's shield and it is said that the winged horse Pegasus sprang from her blood. The sacredness of snakes is shown in the Hopi tribe, who use snakes in their annual Snake Dance. They revere the snakes and hold them in their mouths while they perform this centuries old ritual. Quetzacotl, the plumed serpent god of the Aztecs, was half snake and half bird. Wherever snakes are used as a symbol, the idea of shedding one's skin, death, change, and transformation are implicit.

The bird was another symbol used for the Goddess; the bird represented her spirit. The dove particularly was used because of its gentle, amorous nature. Doves adorned the lunar axes of Crete which were carried in religious procession by the women.[19] In the shrine at the palace of Knossus in Crete, three columns symbolized the moon goddess and her phases, and each column was surmounted by a dove.[20] In early Christianity, the Holy Spirit was depicted as a dove in all of the sacred art. Oak trees were sacred to the Celts of Europe, the Ainu of Japan, and the people of Asia Minor because doves nestled in them.[21]

There are many rituals we can do at this lunation utilizing these various symbols. We can place an eagle feather on the altar and call in the Mayan goddess Ix Chel. We can also place black or both black and white candles on the altar and stones such as smoky quartz, obsidian, and jet. Here is a chant to sing at this time:

May We All Fly Like Eagles
May we all fly like Eagles,
Flying so high,
Circling the universe,
On wings of pure light.

O wi chi tay yo, o we hi yo,
O wi chi tay yo, o we hi yo.

Where we sit is holy,
Holy is the ground,
Forest, mountain, ocean,
Circle us around.

O wi chi tay yo, o we hi yo,
O wi chi tay yo, o we hi yo.

Oh how I love you,
More than words can tell,
Oh how I love you,
And I always will.

O wi chi tay yo, o we hi yo,
o wi chi tay yo, o we hi yo.

(Tape: *In Vision, Songs of Spirit*)

Full Moon in Taurus (*Sun in Scorpio*)

Invocation to Inanna
Inanna, Inanna, Inanna,
Queen of the Heavens,
Lady of the dark moon,
We call upon you, Inanna.

We ask for your courage to die,
We ask for your faith to be reborn,
We ask to go willingly,
into the dark underground.

Inanna, Inanna, Inanna,
Lady of the dark night,
Blessed one of Sumer,
Be with us Inanna.

The full moon in Taurus is very powerful, and rituals for it often involve the use of costumes because of its closeness to All Hallows Eve. With Taurus, we are celebrating earth energies and the sensuousness and beauty of the goddess Aphrodite or Venus. With the sun in Scorpio we are mindful of letting go of old patterns and transforming our desire nature.

For our costumes, we might employ some of the Scorpio symbolism as snakes or serpents, the caduceus (two intertwined snakes), eagle feathers, or feathers of other birds as the owl, who is associated with the Scorpionic energies. We might also utilize the Taurean colors, the green-blue of Venus, stones such as malachite, emerald, aquamarine, turquoise.

Scorpio is the time of the Dark Goddess and our ritual might reflect the wildness, passion, freedom, and ecstasy of the dark goddesses. Some of us may come dressed as Kali, Pele, Hecate, Medusa (with her hair full of snakes), Sekhmet, or Ereshkigal.

We may invoke any of the dark goddesses (see Kali Invocation with the Dark Moon phase, Hecate with Full Moon in Scorpio, Pele with New Moon in Aries, Sekhmet with New Moon in Leo). Inanna and Ereshkigal are the Sumerian goddesses who reflect Taurus/Scorpionic energy. Inanna chose to go into the underground to visit her sister Ereshkigal, who had been stripped of her earthly powers and banished below. In the underground, Inanna was asked to give up her jewels and her clothes and finally, her body was hung upon a peg by her jealous sister. After her death, Inanna was reborn, returned above ground, and assumed her role as the Queen of Sumer. Here is a good chant to use at this lunation:

> We are the old people,
> We are the new people,
> We are the same people,
> Wiser than before.[22]

New Moon in Sagittarius

This lunation occurs between November 21 and December 21, the beginnings of the winter season in the Northern Hemisphere. Sagittarius is represented with the archer and his bow shooting up into the heavens. The archer is a later adaptation of the original feminine representation of this sign, the goddess Artemis. Artemis was goddess of the hunt and ruled the night sky as well. According to the Greek legend, she asked her father Zeus for eternal virginity and a bow and arrow like her brother Apollo's.[23] Artemis was the goddess-priestess of the Amazon communities in Asia Minor and Africa. These were communities of women who hunted, lived alone without men, but were known to be wise and beneficent as rulers. They were noted for the girdles they wore around their waists; these were made of precious metals and stones and served to protect them.

Artemis represents all three aspects of the Goddess—her eternal virginity expresses the virgin or daughter aspect; as the goddess of childbirth she represents the mother; and her gift to bring a swift death (any woman who died quickly was said to be shot by Artemis' arrow) emphasizes the crone. Artemis was also related to the ancient Bear Mother. Often Artemis and her companions assumed the shape of bears and Athenian girls danced as bears in honor of Artemis.[24]

At this time we can decorate our altars with blue-green candles and stones such as turquoise and chrysocolla. We might also have symbols of the crescent moon, representations of Artemis, or other bear mothers.

For our ritual, we may invoke Artemis and experience her courage and strength flowing through us. In our circle, we might share areas in our lives where we need imagination (like the flight of the arrow) to expand our vision or courage to express our ideals in concrete form (hit the target). The warmth and nurture of the Bear Mother embracing us is an experience we may have at this time.

For the invocation to Artemis see Full Moon in Sagittarius.

Full Moon in Gemini (*Sun in Sagittarius*)

This winter full moon takes place between November 21 and December 21 and may fall close to the Winter Solstice. At this full moon we are preparing to celebrate the birth of the year and the sun's increasing light as days begin to grow longer.

The twins represented in the constellation Gemini are Castor and Pollux, equally bright stars in the heavens. Castor and Polydeuces (the Romans changed his name to Pollux) were known in Sparta for their military skills. According to legend, Castor had a mortal father, but Pollux's father was Zeus. Young Spartans who earned these names officiated at religious rites representing the waxing and waning year.[25] They received their royal status after they made love with the Leucippides, the priestesses of Artemis who ruled spring and summer, and those of Athena, who controlled fall and winter.[26] Whenever a new temple was scheduled to be dedicated to the moon, these young men harnessed themselves to a moon chariot and raced to their death, after which their bodies were interred under the temple threshold to ward off hostile influences. The basic symbolism in the story is that the twins were born from the Great Mother or the Cosmic Egg, and represented each half, the waxing and waning. We are told that in prepatriarchal times the constellation Gemini was represented by a woman and a man, not two men.[27]

The meaning of the twins as the two polarities of our being is clear; it is the balance between these polarities that we seek to attain at this lunation. How can we bring our female receptive side into harmony with the male aggressive side, the yin with the yang? This is a question we not only ask personally, but also in terms of the society and the culture in which we live.

We can decorate our altars with agates, tiger's eye, and cat's eye, which are stones having the vibration of the planet Mercury (ruler of the sign Gemini). Yellow candles might also be appropriate as well as representations of the yin/yang polarity. Replicas of Isis and Osiris, Artemis and Apollo, Hera and Zeus, Ishtar and Tammuz symbolize the sexual polarity. Any of these couples may be invoked in our ritual as we share how we are working on the polarities within us and with the opposite sex.

Since both Gemini and Sagittarius are signs of change and movement, the following chant is an appropriate one:

Changing Woman (*Adele Getty*)

There was a time before we were born
When we were the calm in the eye of the storm.
We had a memory oh so deep, about the truth and
　the beauty so sweet.
Man and a woman passion run wild,
They gave birth to a freedom child.

We are the children of love and light,
We will guide the planet through the perilous
　night.

There is a woman who weaves in the sky,
See how she spins, see her fingers fly.
She is the stardust from beginning to end.
She is our mother, our lover, our friend.
She is the weaver and we are the web.
She is the needle and we are the thread.

She changes everything she touches and every
　thing she touches changes,

(Repeat) (*Shekinah Mountain Water*)

We are the flow, we are the ebb, we are the weavers
　and we are the web.

(Repeat)

Changing woman, rearranges. Changing woman,
　rearranges.[28]

ENDNOTES

1. Kealoha, Anna, *Songs of the Earth*, Celestial Arts, Berkeley, 1989. (Songs compiled by Anna Kealoha.)

2. Graves, Robert, *The White Goddess*, Farrar, Straus & Giroux, New York, 1980, p. 166.

3. Kealoha, p. 96.

4. *Ibid.*, p. 157.

5. *Ibid.*, p. 121.

6. *Ibid.*, p. 125.

7. Thorsten, Geraldine, *God Herself*, p. 13.

8. *Ibid.*, p. 4.

9. Kealoha, p. 162.

10. Thorsten, p. 260.

11. *Ibid.*, p. 100.

12. *Ibid.*

13. *Ibid.*

14. Masters, Robert, *The Goddess Sekhmet*, p. 46.

15. Stone, Merlin, *Ancient Mirrors of Womanhood*, p. 85.

16. Kealoha, p. 160.

17. *Ibid.*, p. 128.

18. Stone, p. 93.

19. Clotz, *The Aegean Civilization*, p. 234.

20. *Ibid.*, p. 229.

21. Graves, Robert, *The Greek Myths*, Volume 1, p. 50.

22. Kealoha, p. 175.

23. Graves, p. 83.

24. Gimbutas, Marija, *The Language of the Goddess*, p. 116.

25. Graves, *The Greek Myths*, Volume 1, pp. 250–252.

26. Thorsten, p. 42.

27. *Ibid.*, p. 51.

28. Kealoha, pp. 176–177.

Puberty Ceremonies

"Yellow, red, and orange leaves were falling onto the ground decorating the small plaza. The square was crowded; everybody was dressed in their best clothing. From off in the distance I could hear drumming and the sound of rattles—some older girls and boys were practicing their dances. The splatter of meat roasting over open fires made my stomach tighten with hunger, and the rich smell of bread baking in the great outdoor ovens, mingling with the odor of pinyon smoke, rose up and drifted into the room where my grandmother and mother were fixing my hair and helping me put on my special dress.

It was hard to sit still as they wound my new braids tightly around my head, digging the sharp, pointed ends of the wooden clasps deep into my scalp. I wanted to stamp my foot and cry out, but I knew today I was to become a woman, so I squeezed my nails hard into my palms and kept quiet. How would I like this new way of wearing my hair? My loose hanging braids had been free and flowing; now, with my hair twisted firmly around my head, I felt tied down and formal, not able to turn my head freely. Was this what being a woman was about?

My mother hung a necklace of turquoise beads and coral around my neck, and my grandmother tied the delicate earrings of silver and turquoise to the holes in my ears. Soon, I would go down to the plaza and dance with the others who had already gone through the ritual making them adults. I felt excited and scared. No longer would anyone think of me as a child. I would have less free time and have to work harder like my mother and aunts. I might even get married in a few years and have my own children. Today was the most exciting day in my entire life."

This account of preparing for a puberty ceremony is my own story; it did not actually occur as part of my adolescence, but came to me during a workshop on women's rituals. My friend Edyne Decker drummed and lead all of us women on a journey back to the time when we were ready to experience a puberty rite, something none of us had been given in our own culture. My visual journey was so powerful that I felt I had actually gone through the ceremony in another life. The details were vivid and came to me so easily that they seemed to be something I had already experienced, not something I imagined. I knew I had been in that pueblo; that I was that girl.

As joyful as my visualization of a native puberty rite was, the reality of my own menarche was not nearly as happy, and that of my friend, Alice, was completely miserable. Alice, who grew up an only child in a Jewish American family, had been fascinated when she was around ten years old by the full-page magazine ads featuring a tall model dressed in a strapless satin evening gown. The ad carried the simple legend "Modess because . . . ." Sex was never mentioned by Alice's mother for fear of frightening or distressing her; so Alice decided that such an elegant advertisement could have nothing to do with anything as lowly or taboo as sex. When she asked her mother what Modess was, her mother hemmed and hawed and embarrassedly said, "It's something older girls wear. When you get to be twelve or thirteen, you will bleed every month for a few days from your peepee, and you'll have to wear a gauze bandage between your legs. That's Modess." When Alice asked why this happened to girls, her mother said, "It's a part of growing up. Don't worry. You're still a child yet." Alice didn't dare ask if "it" happened to her mother, and she wondered why she hadn't seen Modess in the linen cupboard where all the medicines and sanitary supplies were kept. She didn't know that her mother, who was considerably older, had just gone through her own menopause, and that the headaches and sweating attacks her mother complained of were not due to Alice's misbehavior as she had been told. One day, just after Alice became eleven, she came home for lunch and discovered a spot of blood on her panties. She told her mother who rushed off to the market to get Modess and a belt. These she brought home, shoved the bag at Alice, and told her to go into the toilet and put them on. When Alice had trouble fastening the pad to the belt her mother bellowed instructions through the closed door. Then she told Alice to return to school and tell no one what had happened. Her mother must have called her father at work, however, because when he came home, he said in a displeased fashion, "Well, Alice, I see now you are a woman." Alice didn't like this idea because it seemed to mean she could no longer be her father's companion, but must somehow become like her mother. Her father added, "Some women complain at this time of the month. Be sure you don't. There is no good reason for complaining. If you don't think about it, you won't feel anything."

In one respect at least, Alice did become like her mother, for when her own girls reached puberty, she handled the matter much as her mother had. She felt ashamed for her daughters. She did explain, as her mother had neglected to do, that the onset of menstruation was connected with a woman's ability to conceive a child, and she added some precautionary rules about sexual conduct. But she did nothing to make the menarche a joyful or even a comprehensible experience for her two daughters.

Today, in Western cultures (other than in practicing Native American groups or in Wicca) the menarche, though treated more gently and sensitively than Alice's or her daughters' was, is usually not honored by ceremony or ritual. The Jewish Bat Mitzvah, which is supposed to represent the girl's becoming a woman in the same way that Bar Mitzvah celebrates the beginning of manhood, has lost its physiological origins. Menarche isn't mentioned, and often more emphasis is placed on an elaborate dinner or party than on the meaning of the event. The bat mitzvah then becomes a social event connecting the girl to her family and religion, but not to the natural cycles of her own body.

Recently certain popular television shows, have tried to stress the importance of the menarche. On "The Cosby Show," one whole episode was devoted to the family's custom of having a mother/daughter day whenever one of the girls first began menstruation. But part of the humor of the program was that the mother/daughter day was met by great resistance from the daughter. "Blossom," another current TV show, had a very poignant episode where Blossom, a girl from an Italian American family whose mother no longer lived with her, didn't know how to tell her father and brothers that she had started menstruating. Instead, Blossom dreamed that the mother on "The Cosby Show" was her mother who spent that very important day with her answering questions and participating in "girl talk."

Another positive sign that times are changing and that women in the United States are getting input from other cultures can be seen in an article in the July 15, 1991, *New York Times*, Metropolitan Section. A young women from Ghana is shown dressed in the costume of her country, seated with her hands on her knees facing outward, while at her back, older women, also ritually dressed, are dancing, singing, and drumming. The accompanying article states that the young Ghanaian woman, now attending the North Academic Center at City College in Harlem, was celebrating the traditional coming-of-age ceremony of the Akan tribe. "Gifts of food, soaps, perfumes, and bolts of Ghanaian cloth were spread in silver bowls before the young woman. A

few feet away, the Bragorofuo, a dozen or so of her female elders, chanted and sang songs imparting age-old womanly advice . . . . The female elders awoke the young woman at 5 A.M. to bathe her, signifying her passage from child to woman. Then the elders accompanied her throughout the day, talking and singing about a woman's responsibilities—and about men."[1] The end of the article states that the coming-of-age ceremony is rarely performed in the United States, and now is performed less and less in Ghana due to the spread of Christianity. Hopefully, this article will inspire other young women, not necessarily Ghanaian, to consider the possibility of celebrating their own coming-of-age.

Ritual and ceremony are spiritual ways to help a young woman cross over the threshold to adulthood. Today, girls become nubile as early as eight or nine and as late as fifteen or sixteen, so rituals must be tailored to the age of the girl. Also, the year before the onset of menstruation is usually one of heightened sensitivity and emotionality because hormonal balances change. Parents and schools need to be aware of the great differences between girls who nonetheless all go through the same ultimate experience. Preparation for the menarche should occur from early childhood so that a girl's first bleeding is anticipated with pride and joy and is understood and respected by all persons in the young woman's life.

Tribal Puberty Customs

In all tribal cultures, the beginning of menstruation is an important time for a young woman. She is taught about the role of women in her tribe; she is prepared for marriage and told what her role will be afterward. She is often given an elaborate initiation ceremony which may last for four days or even a full month in some tribes. There is more information available about girls' puberty ceremonies than about any other rite of passage in native society. In the Navajo religion, which has many types of Sings and Blessingways, the puberty ceremony is considered the most important ritual.[2] Not only does it ensure the health, prosperity, and well-being of the maiden, but the ceremony is symbolic as well. The maiden honored represents Changing Woman and the reproductive cycle. Her personal coming-of-age is connected to the growth of plants and the fertility of the Earth Mother.[3]

The Navajo ceremony of Kinaaldá demonstrates the transformational quality of the puberty ceremony through the practice of "molding." In molding, with the intent of enhancing the attractiveness of the girl, a woman attendant molds the girl in order to press her body into conformity with what the Navajos considered was a good figure. The Navajo religion believes that the beautiful and good are the same in meaning. For the Navajo, body molding affects the girl's personality and essence as well as her exterior beauty.[4]

When a girl first begins to bleed, she is usually sent to a small hut or tipi isolated from the rest of the tribe. Her food is brought to her by other women, but she is not allowed to eat either salt or meat. In some tribes, she actually fasts with nothing but water. She is also not allowed to scratch her head or her hair will fall out, so she is given a special scratching stick.[5] In most North American Indian tribes, four days and nights were spent in the menstrual hut, after which the maiden was bathed in cold water by her mother and allowed to reenter the home.

After her time in the moon hut, dances and celebrations were held in her honor, often for a month afterwards. Maria Chona, a Papago woman, reports on the Papago ceremonies. Dances were held every night for one entire moon cycle. She writes how tired she got from dancing every night and then working hard all day getting wood and preparing food.[6] When the rites were completed, she was bathed and taken to a medicine man to be cleansed and given a new name.

One of the seven rites of the Lakotas is the Puberty Blessing Songs (Isna Ti Alowan). *Isna Ti* means "living alone" or being temporarily isolated during menstruation.[7] How a young woman behaved at the time of her puberty was believed to shape her disposition and attitude. Industriousness and modesty were two traits that were extolled. She was encouraged to work hard at this time, practice silence, and not look directly at people's faces. She was also instructed in her life's goals, including the primary one of old age. It was believed that a young woman who had this ceremony was more likely to attain old age than one who did not have it.[8]

One of the most important concepts behind the puberty rites was the idea of power. Most tribal people believe that a menstruating woman has power to affect others; that is the reason why there are so many taboos regarding food, dishes, and medicine objects touched by menstruating females. They believed that women

and pubescent girls during their menstrual time could cure and heal. The Apache explain that a pubescent girl is like a medicine man; she can cure and also help to bring rain.[9]

The most difficult part of understanding or emulating native puberty rites for us today relates to the taboos that were enforced. Taboos varied among the tribes but they had many similarities. One of the taboos forbade a girl from scratching herself with her fingernails or her hair would fall out, her face would become covered with black streaks, or her body become scarred.[10] The Navajo idea of body molding would be abhorrent or impossible for many Westerners to understand or try to imitate even though Western medicine finds no fault with surgical alteration of a women's body to conform to current beauty standards. The difference between the Navajo practice and today's surgical or hormonal interference is that the Navajo believes molding transforms the inner being as well as the outer.

Another taboo concerned the drinking of water. In some tribes the initiate could only drink through a hollow straw or through a reed. For the Tlingits living in southern Alaska, this straw had to be made from the wing bone of a white headed eagle.[11] The Tlingits also isolated the girl from the village for a whole year; she could leave her hut only at night and had to wear a broad brimmed hat so as not to taint the stars with her gaze.[12]

The Yumas in Arizona had taboos against talking to prevent garrulousness; laughing to prevent light-headedness; and bathing, to prevent loss of strength.[13] Other tribes did not allow pubescent girls to touch any sacred objects, shields, or war objects for fear that they would taint them.[14] They were also not allowed to eat fresh meat because of the fear of future unavailability of game.[15]

In addition to the taboos, there were many rituals that the girls had to undergo for certain time periods. In the Chinook tribe in Washington, a girl had to bathe every day for five months following her first menses to ensure future strength and regular occurrence of the menses.[16] This was not easy during the cold wet winter. In the Fox tribe, during the ritual bath, the skin on a girl's back and sides were pricked until she bled freely to ensure that she would not have an excessively heavy menstrual flow.[17]

Although these taboos are not practical or desirable to incorporate into today's puberty rites, other native ways and ideas are. Many cultures expected the young girl to establish an identification with a particular goddess or sacred object. The young woman would carry this identification beyond its ritual context so as to infuse all her future actions with meaning. Puberty initiation was often a celebration of creativity; of women's role as bearers of children, raisers of crops, providers of food, sustainers of life, and sources of imaginative and intuitive powers. When the girl at menarche was given symbolic items such as clothing or jewelry, had songs chanted in her behalf, myths retold for her benefit, or had paintings placed on her body, she not only was initiated into womanhood, but into the cosmic order as well.[18]

There were many joyous aspects to puberty rites, as in the Papago ceremony mentioned above and in the Apache and Navajo ceremonies. The Apaches credit White Painted Woman with establishing the puberty rite. Her son is often associated with her in this rite.[19] The Navajos speak of Changing Woman as the one who set the precedent for the *Kinaaldá*, which is what the Navajos call the puberty ceremony. An excerpt from the origins of the *Kinaaldá* says, "the ceremony was started so women would be able to have children and the human race would be able to multiply. To do this, women had to have relations with men. The Kinaaldá was created to make it holy and effective, as the Holy People wanted it to be."[20]

Keith Basso lived on the Cibecue Apache reservation in Arizona. In 1960 and 1961 he observed the puberty rite that is known as *Na ih es*. He reports that it was a big decision for a family to sponsor this celebration as it involves much time in planning and preparation and quite a bit of money. The parents select a group of elders who will be the sponsors; these elders are in charge of choosing the location or dance ground which must be close to wood and water and have a large space for the dance area. They then select a medicine man to sing the *Na ih es*. For four or five nights prior to the ceremony, social dances are held. The day prior to the ceremony there is a sweat bath for all the male relatives after which the medicine man makes the ritual paraphernalia for the ceremony. The relatives prepare the food and at dusk the girl is dressed up in her ritual garments. Twelve songs are sung by the medicine man and the girl dances on a piece of buckskin. She is presented with the ritual paraphernalia which includes a wooden staff or cane to which an eagle feather and turquoise bead are attached, also

four ribbons (black, green, yellow, and tan) to symbolize the four directions. She is given a scratching stick and drinking tube, both of which she must use for four days after the ceremony. She is also given an abalone shell pendant. She wears a special buckskin serape and dances on a large piece of buckskin. The ceremony itself is divided into eight parts. The first part comprises eight to twelve songs which are creation songs. In the second part, the impregnation of Changing Woman by the sun is sung. The girl is massaged in the third part so that her body will become strong. The fourth and fifth sections are similar; the cane is placed in the ground and she runs to it symbolizing her four stages of life. If she falls, she has to begin that stage again. In the fifth section, she runs to the four directions. The medicine man sprinkles corn and candy over the girl in the sixth part, and all the relatives run up to catch some. In the seventh section, she is blessed with holy powder and the relatives also repeat the blessing for themselves. In the last section, four songs are sung by the medicine man; then the girl steps off the buckskin, picks it up, shakes it, and throws it to the east. She then throws a blanket in each of the other directions. For the following four days, the girl stays at the dance ground with her family. She is not allowed to wash, can drink only through the tube, and can not touch herself except with the scratching stick. Her power is considered strong enough during these four days to heal the sick or to bring rain.[21]

Physical Preparation for Puberty Today

Preparing young girls for puberty so that they will not be upset when they begin their menses is one of the most important acts a mother can perform for her daughter. Young girls need to understand that to become a woman and bleed every month is a beautiful experience, not "the curse." Our culture has programmed a negative view of the monthly moon cycle through its advertisements for pills, potions, tampons, and "stay-free" pads. When I was growing up in the 1950s I remember advertisements such as "Mary's blue with her monthly period; Mary's bright with Midol." Or "Use Anacin for those monthly cramps." This type of programming instills fears and misunderstanding in young women before they even have the experience of their first bleeding.

In our society, girls are encouraged to detach themselves from their bodies and to regard any change as an inconvenience or illness. Neglected, menstruation often becomes a sickness whose language is discomfort and anger. In other languages the majority of words for menstruation are synonymous with the sacred, the spiritual, the supernatural, or the deity.[22] It is sad that one of the most basic experiences in the life of a woman is one of the most ignored.

If a young girl is healthy, has been eating and exercising well, there is no need for her to have physical symptoms such as cramps. However, it is a good idea as a girl reaches puberty, to begin mineral, vitamin, and herbal supplements so that her body can remain in balance through the hormonal changes that are starting. Often acne and other skin conditions develop and can be controlled through the addition of supplements and herbs and the regulation of diet. Tribal cultures did not have the same problems with foods that we have because everything they ate was "organic," free of chemicals, and was prepared in a simple, healthy way.

I believe it is very important to help the young girl understand what food does to her body so she can decide how she wants to prepare for a beautiful puberty and womanhood. If she is educated to know the value of whole grains and vegetables and fruits, and isn't fed "junk foods," she can begin to gain some insight into the possibility of aligning her body with Mother Nature or the Goddess. She will understand the relationship between the beauty and purity of nature and the beauty and balance of her own physical self. She can begin to love her body and its cycles of bleeding and ovulation, and not resent menstruation or try to hide it.

Supplements such as magnesium, potassium, and calcium are most important for hormonal changes: magnesium for preventing cramping, potassium for healthy skin, and calcium for growth of bones and teeth. Minerals such as zinc for the immune system and skin and iron for the loss of blood are also important. Important vitamins are: Bioflavonoids for general health and circulation of the blood, the B vitamins (especially B-6 for hormonal changes), and vitamin E. A good multi-vitamin mineral may be used along with the above additions.

Raspberry leaf tea is a general female toner that helps to balance the body and is high in magnesium; sarsaparilla root is another good female herb which is also a blood purifier. Mix sarsaparilla root with dandelion root, 1 teaspoon of each to 1-1/2 cups of water and simmer for a pleasant tea. Dandelion root helps balance the blood sugar which often becomes low when one starts to menstruate.

The Chinese herb dong quai has been used very successfully for young girls at the onset of menses. Dong quai is readily available in health food stores (as are other herbs and roots) and can be simmered with some Chinese licorice and made into a tea. If this is drunk a few times weekly, menstrual flow should be regular and there should not be much cramping. Camomile, catnip, scullcap, and spearmint are nervine teas that are relaxing for the system if one has cramps. Vervain is also a good female herb and can be mixed with any of the above nervines.

For delayed menstruation, uterine tonics can be helpful. Blue cohosh, chasteberry (known as vitex), false unicorn root, and rue are good uterine tonics. They can be mixed together in equal parts and simmered with a few cups of water. A few cups may be taken every other day.

Massage and foot massage are also wonderful tools for girls to learn; they can work on each other's bodies and help themselves feel in balance. This can also help them get in tune with each part of their physique and to begin to enjoy their bodies. Foot massage is called reflexology; every community usually has a person working with reflexology who can help the young girl understand the correspondences between various areas of the foot and parts of the body. Using oils and lotions to keep the skin moist and healthy is another way to work with the body. Massage is a skill all girls would enjoy learning, practicing, and receiving.

Emotional Preparation

In addition to balancing her body, it is important to instruct pubescent girls on the meaning of the monthly cycle, so that they not only understand their physiology, but they can approach menstruation as a gift of womanhood, a special experience each month, giving them time to rest and relax and enjoy a change from their ordinary activities. In many cultures, menstrual blood was a source of creative inspiration—it was part of the natural cycle by which new life is created. If a new life isn't formed during one particular cycle, then the woman can use the time of her menses for creative thought and work. In Greece, menstrual blood was the "supernatural red wine" given by Hera to the gods. In India, Kali invited the gods "to bathe in the bloody flow of her womb and drink." The Norse god, Thor, owed his enlightenment and eternal life to bathing in a river of menstrual blood. Odin was made powerful by stealing the "wise blood from the mother goddess's triple cauldron and drinking it."[23] Often, during her menstrual time, a woman is open to having dreams which can guide or lead her in creative ways of utilizing her life.

If a girl is instructed on what it means to be a woman—her power and role as the carrier of the mysteries of birth and death and the gift and responsibility of motherhood—she will have less physical discomfort each month and more emotional stability. In addition, there would be fewer unwanted pregnancies because she would understand her responsibility as a woman and the importance of not becoming pregnant unless she is able to care for the child. Most young girls, for example, are often unaware that they can become pregnant while bleeding. They are also not taught by their mothers or in school about natural birth control or temperature and mucus checks that allow them to follow their bodily rhythms. In most homes, a girl's first menstruation is kept quiet; it is not made public and is not considered a time for rejoicing or celebrating.

One of the reasons why the onset of puberty is not greeted by ceremony or ritual in our society is the fear of female sexuality. Many parents are intimidated by the fact that their little girl is now capable of conceiving; they are also forced to think of her as a person with sexual desires. Female sexuality is a powerful force, one that a girl or woman should be aware of and learn to use and control. If this subject is not broached or is shunned, women grow up not understanding their power or misusing it. A woman's deep sense of herself is rooted in the congruence between her mind and body. If a girl understands the power of her sexuality, she will not be driven by a desire to use it for conquest or power, but simply realize her own strength and the important role women play in the stabilization and creation of society.

Modern Puberty Rites

Puberty rites, like rites for menopause, are usually performed with only women present; however, initiation at puberty can be beneficial to society as a whole.

Certainly, a girl's father, grandfather, brothers, and other male relatives should be educated and included in some part of the celebration of female puberty rites. One reason for their participation is that it will teach men to understand and respect a woman's body and "that time of the month." Also, the girl will experience positive male support and acceptance of her new capacity.

Puberty ceremonies may be done soon after the first menstruation; the new moon following menstruation is a good time or, if the ritual is being done for several girls, a ceremony might be done at a special time of the year, such as in the spring, when plants begin to bloom. We often do a ritual for a group of girls under the sign of Taurus (April 22–May 21), since Taurus is the time we celebrate May Day and fertility rites.

Depending on individual family circumstances and the age of the girl who has attained puberty, the ceremony might be a simple one involving just the girl and her mother or, perhaps, a few close relatives. Before the ceremony, it is a good idea to make (or purchase) a special robe or dress that can also be worn for other rituals. Friends can contribute special jewelry. Often a wreath or headdress is made. An altar should always be constructed containing those objects that are sacred to the girl. Her mother or other women can help her learn the qualities of various goddesses, as well as animals and plants, so she can place on her altar those that speak most meaningfully to her.

In a simple ceremony, the four directions can be called on and (if more than two people are present) a circle cast. For this type of simple ceremony, Luisah Teish's explanation of the directions might be used.[24] According to Teish, one calls in the east as the throne of air. The women breathe deeply and ask for pure thoughts and inspiration, visualize clouds, wind, and feathers. Something white is placed in that direction. The south is the throne of fire. The light is called upon, the flame of passion, the flow of blood, the spirit of dancing energy are invoked. The warmth of candlelight and fireplaces, the heat that emanates from the soul is felt. Ask for courage, innocence, and power. Place something red in that direction. The west is the throne of water. Beckon the great wave. Feel deep sleep, the depth of intuition, the waters of the womb. Listen for the ocean's roar through a seashell. Surrender to the tide of love. Place something blue in that direction. The north is the throne of the earth. Introduce the power of the great provider; stamp heavily on the solid earth beneath your feet. Ask for stability, productivity, and abundance. Place something yellow in that direction.

If the puberty ceremony involves more than the immediate family, preparations can be more elaborate. If the mother belongs to a lodge or clan, the members are usually present. Often the girl is then inducted into the lodge or forms a lodge with other girls her own age. Again, the girl is decked in a special robe and jewels. A circle is cast, preferably outdoors. In the middle of the circle, an altar should be made with objects for the four directions, mother goddess figures, flowers and herbs, cornmeal in a bowl, ice cold water in a chalice or goblet, three veils or scarves (preferably white, red, and black) and any gifts. Adding the wish c rd from the Tarot (the nine of cups or the nine of vessels) is symbolically significant. The Native American Tarot deck connects the nine of vessels (cups) with puberty rites. It shows a maid kneeling on a robe, wearing a traditional ceremonial puberty dress. Cattail pollen, a holy substance, is showered as a blessing by a well-wisher. Three trees are tied together in symbolic protection over the participants. The wish is for a long and happy life; sympathetic magic is used to ward off famine and evil, both from the young girl and from her entire tribe, all of whom recognize the power of menstrual blood. The wish card in any Tarot deck (or the nine of hearts in a standard deck of cards) represents the awakening of new emotions and a new outlook on life. Often if the nine of pentacles or shields (diamonds) is added, the fulfillment of the wish is promised.

For the ceremony, each of the girls should be dressed by her mother and grandmother, if possible, and any other close relatives and friends. At the beginning of the rite, everyone is smudged with cedar or sage or some other incense and the space is purified. The girl sits in the east and is blindfolded. The women in the circle form a line facing the east and spread their legs. The maiden then crawls through this tunnel which symbolizes the birth channel or transformation. The women may poke, tickle, or prod the initiate as she goes through the tunnel. The last woman in the line is her mother, who will take her from the tunnel into the center of the circle. There, one of the women waits with a bowl of icy cold water which is splashed gently into the girl's face as the blindfold is removed. (Interesting how conventional religious ceremonies reenact ancient rites. This splashing is reminiscent of the Catholic bishop slapping the face of each participant during confirmation at age thirteen.) The splashing in the puberty rite represents the shock of birth. The initiate is then welcomed into the circle and hugged by all the women.

The initiate's mother or one of the other women presents her to the four directions. The following cross-cultural invocations to each the four directions may be used:

O Spirits of the East, the place of new beginnings, bless this maiden as she begins her journey to womanhood. Help her to learn the lessons of the east, to sustain her vision, to maintain lofty ideals like the eagle. Grandmothers and grandfathers of the eastern gate, protect and bless this woman as she enters her new phase.

The mother or another woman then turns the girl and presents her to the south:

O Ancient Ones of the South, Goddess Pele, who has the volcanic power of tne south, bless this maiden and teach her the love, the warmth, the intensity of the south. Help her to learn the lessons of the heart, faith, and humility and withstand the fires of the emotions. Grandmothers and grandfathers of the southern gate, protect and bless this woman as she enters her new phase.

Next, the girl is presented to the west:

O Spirits of the West, home of Changing Woman, the deep, dark, watery place. Bless this maiden and teach her the lessons of the west—the introspection and transformation she will go through on her path to becoming a woman. Bring in the black bear to protect her and heal her when she faces the dark. Grandmothers and grandfathers of the western gate, protect and bless this woman as she enters her new phase.

A fourth woman, or the girl's mother presents her to the north:

Ancestors of the North, ancient healing ones, be with this maiden and bless her. Teach her of your old ways and traditions, the wisdom of

White Buffalo Woman. Allow her to experience the cold and the snow and the winds of the north as she grows into womanhood. Grandmothers and grandfathers of the northern gate, protect and bless this woman as she enters her new phase.

Now, she is presented to Earth Mother and Sky Father (in Wiccan ritual she would be taken to the center of the circle and presented to the Lady and Lord, or to the Great Goddess).

After the maiden (or maidens) is taken to each direction, she sits in the center where one woman takes cornmeal from the bowl and makes a cornmeal circle around her. This is a symbol of fertility, and the woman putting the cornmeal around may call in the corn maiden, or Demeter or Ceres, the great corn mothers. She may ask for the fertility and health of the young maiden, that she might grow into womanhood, and herself become a mother.

Next, three women enter who are dressed in one of the three veils. These women represent the three phases of the Goddess and each speaks to the maidens.

The first one lifts her white veil and says:

I am the eternal maiden within you born from the morning dew. I am full of promise and hopes to come. I am the innocent child within you, giving you the ability to see with clarity and purpose. I will always be there with you as your virgin self, even as you grow closer to my sisters, the mother and the crone. You may always call on me when you need to get in touch with these qualities.

The second one lifts her red veil and speaks:

I am Gaia, the Mother Goddess, the rich green earth. You see me alive everywhere—in the plants, the animals, the rocks, the rivers, the mountains. As the mother, I give birth to the seeds conceived by the maiden. I nourish these seeds and water them so that they may grow strong. As a young woman, you have the power of the mother within you, to nurture your own ideas and projects. As you grow and learn, you will use this power in the mundane world and in the spirit world. Remember that the love of the mother is always within you, and through pain, joy, tears and laughter, you will find me within your heart.

Then the crone speaks through her black veil, lifting it only slightly.

I am the crone within you, the ageless wisdom of nature. I am the winter that comes after the blossoms of spring and fruitfulness of summer. I am barren but I am also beautiful as the white snow that covers the ground. I hold the keys to the underworld and understand the mysteries of death. I am change and sacrifice and the transformation that comes after the sacrifice. I represent both birth and death in my infinite wisdom. I am with you always and you may always call on me.

After the three women leave the circle, all gather around the maiden and a cup of wine, grape or cherry juice (symbolizing the blood) is sipped by all in the circle. The maiden drinks first. While they are passing the cup around, the maiden reads the following poem:

Daughter Chant
(*From the Navajo Puberty Ceremony*)

Watch over me.
Hold your hand before me in protection.
Stand guard for me, speak in defense of me.
As I speak for you, so do ye.
As you speak for me, thus shall I do.

May it be beautiful before me.
May it be beautiful behind me.
May it be beautiful below me.
May it be beautiful above me.
May it be beautiful around me.

I am restored in beauty.
I am restored in beauty.
I am restored in beauty.
I am restored in beauty.[25]

As each woman drinks, she says a prayer or blessing for the maiden or maidens. Then gifts are shared and special family gifts are presented by the mother. Everyone in the circle shares stories of her own puberty ceremony (if she had one), and gives advice on herbs and other practical suggestions. Food is served, including corn bread and other festive foods. All foods and the first drop of liquid in the cup are offered first to the Earth Mother.

Sometimes a cone of power is formed where the women line up around each maiden and lift her into the air, chanting her spiritual name as they do so. They rock her back and forth and bless her, before returning her to the earth. This can be done before drinking the grape juice or wine.[26] (Some variations of this ceremony have the maiden naked and then the women put mud on her body to show the change she is going through. Afterwards the mud is washed off and her body is bathed ceremonially.) After the ceremony is completed, male relations can be included for pot luck or feasting.

Obviously, it is important to utilize a ceremony that is appropriate both to the girl and to the adults who are participating. The celebrants should be carefully selected, and the rituals designed to have meaning for the girl and her family. A ceremony for a younger girl (between eight and ten) should be simple and offer a gentle introduction into the lodge of womanhood. For older girls, the maturing sexuality of the initiate can be stressed. Here the pubescent girl is more ready to act as a woman in all phases of her life. In general, the idea that women walk in beauty, in harmony with nature, and with their own bodies is paramount. It is part of a woman's birthright to celebrate through ritual her feminine nature.

Two chants are often used for puberty ceremonies:

Open My Body
Open my body to the rainbow of heaven.
Open my mind to the knowing within.
Open my spirit to the manifest power.
Open my heart to the love all around.

(Tape: *Cycles of Truth*,
Singing Awake, The Dream
by Rashani. Medicine Song
Productions, 156 Sullivan Street,
New York, NY 10012.)

This Is the Goddess in Me
This body, this temple, this is the Goddess in me.
This mind, this light, this is the Goddess in me.
This heart, this altar, this is the Goddess in me.
This breath, this spirit, this is the Goddess in me.

(Tape: see above)

ENDNOTES

1. New York Times, July 15, 1991, B2.

2. Frisbee, Charlotte, *Kinaalda: A Study of the Navajo Girl's Puberty Ceremony*, p. 9.

3. *Ibid.*, p. 373.

4. Shuttle, Penelope, and Redgrave, Peter, *The Wise Wound*, Bantam Books, 1990, p. 311.

5. Frisbee, p. 217.

6. *Ibid.*, p. 220.

7. La Pointe, James, *Legends of the Lakota*, p. 129.

8. *Ibid.*, p. 223.

9. Basso, Kenneth, *Girl's Puberty Ceremony*, pp. 53–72.

10. Niethammer, *Daughters of the Earth*, p. 39.

11. *Ibid.*

12. *Ibid.*

13. *Ibid.*, p. 40.

14. Beck & Walters, *The Sacred*, p. 222.

15. Niethammer, p. 50.

16. *Ibid.*

17. *Ibid.*

18. Lincoln, Bruce, *Emerging from the Chrysalis*, Howard University Press, 1981, p. 104.

19. Beck & Walters, p. 227.

20. Frisbee, p. 11.

21. Basso, Keith, *The Gift of Changing Woman*.

22. Shuttle and Redgrave, p. 311.

23. Buckley and Gottlieb, p. 311.

24. Teish, Luisah, *Jambalaya*, Harper & Row, San Francisco, 1985, p. 241.

25. Washburn, Penelope, ed., *Seasons of Woman*, pp. 20–21.

26. This and other ideas for this ceremony are from The Grove of Phoenix Rising, P.O. Box 43586, Austin, TX 78745.

Marriage

Marriage may well be the most important rite of passage in a woman's life—a time when she makes a commitment to bond with another being and set up a home for herself and her partner, a time perhaps to look forward to motherhood—a time of total change.

The ceremony that marks the marriage rite of passage is one that should be carefully thought out and prepared. In fact, marriage doesn't just involve a one-time ceremony; it is an ongoing commitment which deepens over time. This commitment may be enacted through a ritual five or ten years later or whenever the couple feel they are entering another level in their relationship. One woman who attended our women's rituals workshops related that she and her husband had a ceremony eight years after their marriage because it was only then that they realized the depth of their commitment.

There is also a need for ritual at the time of a divorce or a severing of the partnership, either with the couple together or with the individuals separately. To acknowledge that the relationship has reached a point where the individuals involved can no longer grow together is to acknowledge that there has been growth in the relationship and that a turning point has been reached. Having each individual do a ritual and cut old cords with the other person leaves her/him freer to pursue a new direction. This is, in itself, like marriage, a significant rite of passage.

In many Native American tribes, there were months of elaborate preparations before a marriage ceremony took place. Goods were exchanged and often the couple spent time at each other's homes performing services and getting to know the family.

In the Hopi tradition the ceremony was the responsibility of the bride and the female relatives of the bride and groom. The bride began the preparations first by grinding corn and making *piki* (a thin wafer bread) at her mother's home, then going to her future mother-in-law's home and spending three days grinding corn and making piki bread from dawn until late at night. This was not only to demonstrate her competence but also to compensate her future mother-in-law for the loss of her son's services around the house. On the fourth morning the bride's female relatives came to the groom's house bringing all the cornmeal and piki bread the bride had prepared there. The groom's female relatives came too, and the two mothers washed their heads in one basin, twisting the hair of the couple into one strand to unite them for life. When their hair

was dry the couple went to the edge of the mesa to pray to the rising sun. After the wedding breakfast, the bridegroom and his relatives descended to the *kiva* (an underground ceremonial chamber) and began to weave the bride's wedding garments. They wove two white wedding robes and a long belt. While they were doing this, the bride remained with her mother-in-law grinding corn and doing other housework to pay for her outfit. The wedding garments were most important because at death a Hopi woman's body was wrapped in the small wedding robe and tied with the belt. The robe became the wings to carry her soul to the House of the Dead and the belt guided her spirit.[1]

In many countries it is traditional to wear wedding garments that have been in the family for generations. In Rumania these traditional clothes are worn by both the bride and groom; everyone else dresses up as well and they all walk to and from the church as part of the celebration. In India in traditional Hindu weddings, the bride's hair and make up is done a certain way and she is given special jewels from her family to wear which she then keeps throughout her life.

Preparations

Preparations are very important. They include the making or choosing of wedding garments, finding the place or site of the ceremony, selecting the person to perform the ceremony, designing and sending out the invitations, and selecting the rings (if they are being used). All of these actions convey the basic purpose or intention of the union. I know a couple who chose not to use the word "wedding" or "marriage" because of its old connotations. They called their ceremony a "joining ceremony." Instead of giving each other individual rings, someone made a huge cornmeal ring or circle around the whole group (it was an outdoor wedding) that symbolized their union was not only with each other but with their friends and community.

The clothes we choose are important for their vibrational quality. Something ancient and ceremonial from family or friends may bring additional meaning to the ceremony. Also significant is a garment that is made specially for the ceremony so that the color, design, and material are carefully thought out. Buying an expensive wedding gown or dress that is worn only once is impractical and often has nothing of our own personality or vibration. Having friends sew on the garment or embroider something special makes the garment a treasured ceremonial dress or robe in which to celebrate other important rites of passage.

Equally important is the site or place. For those of us who desire an outdoor wedding, some place in nature that is a power place for us might be one we choose, or a special ritual site, a beautiful beach, mountain top, or meadow. I have conducted weddings for people at very powerful places—one beach in particular during a ferocious rain and lightening storm. After a quick ritual (done in our rain slickers) the rest of the wedding, including the full ceremony, was moved to a house. Nature provides us with many lessons and adds to the power and the meaning of the ceremony if we choose an outdoor site.

Indoor sites can also be beautiful. Some people love the vibration of a certain church or temple, but they don't want a ceremony done by the minister or rabbi who practices there; they want to rent the place and bring in their own spiritual leader or guide. Others have a specific ashram or worship place where they want to be married. And, of course, many people prefer their own home or a friend's home which may have a special garden, fireplace, or altar.

Perhaps the most important preparation is the choosing of the person or persons who will conduct the ceremony. Whether this person is a spiritual guide, a medicine teacher, a minister, or a personal friend makes no difference as long as the couple feel close to her (or him) and can work out a ceremony that reflects their own intention and desires. Anyone can perform a wedding ceremony that is legally binding as long as the couple takes out an official marriage license that is then signed by the person performing the ceremony. I have seen an infinite variety of ceremonies performed by Native Americans, Hindu gurus, Tibetan lamas, new age rabbis, enlightened ministers, pagans, gypsies, and by groups of friends where there was no one person officiating. The ceremonies were all deep and powerful because the couple had chosen the person(s) and worked with her/him/them to produce a meaningful ritual.

It is essential for anyone performing a marriage ceremony to spend time with the couple, understanding their needs, intentions, anxieties, and the type of ceremony they want. Discussing what they want to say to each other in the ceremony, the writing of their vows, musical interludes, individual contributions, participation by family and friends, are all very rewarding.

The Ceremony
Preparation on Day of Ceremony

The site or place of the ritual needs to be prepared. The place, whether indoors or out, should be smudged with cedar, sage, or some purifying incense as frankincense or sandalwood. An altar should be set up with everything needed for the ceremony, including the marriage license if there is one. If this is a Native American or pagan ceremony, objects would be placed in the four directions. Special crystals chosen by the couple would be on the altar and also some flowers.

Several people should be in charge of welcoming guests as they arrive. Guests may be smudged, blessed with incense, taken to their seats, or lead to a place where they will wait for a processional walk to the site of the ritual. While they are waiting, there should be some music—possibly a flute or other instrument or drumming and rattling by the guests, or recorded music.

Once the guests are situated at the ritual site, the couple should be brought in. They may walk hand in hand together; they may come in separately with their parents or other relatives or friends, or they may come in alone. At one wedding I performed, four different people called in the directions. As they were calling in the directions, one partne. came in at the east, the grown children of each of the partners came in at the south, the other partner at the west, and the parents of the couple came in at the north (the direction of wisdom and the elders). At another ceremony I attended, the couple walked in together carrying a buffalo robe, which they placed in the center of the circle and sat on. At still another ceremony performed by a Native American medicine person, the couple was taken to each of the four directions holding a wedding vase which has two openings; at each direction the medicine man said certain prayers.

Selena Fox, in an article describing a pagan wedding, has the couple move to each of the compass points. In the north, the physical realm, the place of the element earth, she has them place their hands on a pentacle of salt, a dish of soil, or a platter with a round loaf of bread. Here she blesses them with good health, a happy home, groundedness, and fertility. For the element air, she takes them to the east, the mental realm, and blesses them by smudging them with incense or with a feather or by ringing a bell. Here the prayers are for wisdom, good communication, intellectual growth, and knowledge. In the south, the element fire, the action realm, she holds a candle or wand above them. Their marriage is blessed here with creativity, harmony, vitality, and sensuality. For the element water, she takes them to the west, the emotional realm, and blesses them by anointing them with water from a chalice or bowl. The wishes here are for understanding, emotional support, intuition, and friendship. When the four directions are completed, she circles the altar clockwise one time in the center. In the center, the spiritual realm, their foreheads are anointed with a special oil and a crystal or other spiritual symbol is held above them. Here they are blessed with balance, wholeness, integrity, and spiritual growth.[2]

The Ritual

Every ceremonial ritual for a marriage or joining of two people should have the following parts:

1. Some kind of greeting or welcoming by the person or persons performing the ceremony.
2. An invocation, calling in of some spiritual presence, whether it be the Goddess, Buddha, the Spirits of the four directions.
3. Inspirational reading of poetry or talk by the High Priestess, Minister, Medicine person.
4. Music selected by the couple to set the mood for the vows.
5. Contributions by guests of statements, poetry, songs.
6. Statements of the couple to each other.
7. Vows which are read by the person performing the ceremony and repeated by each partner. These vows are usually written beforehand by the couple themselves.
8. Exchanging rings if they are used.
9. Pronouncement of the union by the High Priestess/Priest or Minister.
10. Singing, dancing, and celebration by the group.

Welcome

Here are two examples of a welcome. (The first I wrote and the second was written by a friend of mine at a wedding he and his wife performed.)

We are gathered here today at this very special place to celebrate the marriage of _____ and_____, both of whom have worked together through the years to arrive at the place where they are ready to make their union a permanent partnership, one that will be as deep as the ocean and as solid as the earth we sit on. Marriage is a special kind of commitment; it is gentle like the wind, strong like the sun, and flowing like the river. It is a way of sharing love to the very depths one's heart can hold. This is a time when _____ and _____ wish to acknowledge that they are an extension of the great mystery and all they do together from this day forth will be their conscious commitment to heal each other and to heal Gaia, our great Earth Mother.

_____ and _____ have asked you to be here with them today to share in this celebration of their love, on this wedding day that they have chosen to stand at the beginning of their marriage together. But before they join us, let's take a few moments for ourselves just now to go within and to become aware of the breath we breathe, and of the connection between the earth and the sky that our breath maintains. For breathing deeply of the sky we can feel ourselves gently lifted, and letting that breath go, we can then feel a settling back into the earth. And with this flowing breath of earth and sky within, we also feel the pulse of the constant heart, the source of life and the center of ourselves. It is here we ask that we might be open to ourselves, and to the source and center of all love, that this day might be for each of us a bringing together and a blending, and a healing of all separations in true marriage.[3]

Invocations

There are many types of invocations that are used in marriage ceremonies. In Native American ceremonies, the four directions or six directions (including Earth Mother and Sky Father) are used. Pagans also call in the four directions and then evoke the Goddess, or divine female principle, and God, or divine male principle. Christians often evoke Father/Mother/God which could be expressed as well as Mother/Father/Goddess.

After calling in the six directions, I like to invoke the goddess Aphrodite or Venus, the goddess of love.

I call on the Goddess Aphrodite, be present with your love and bless this couple. Bless their union, make it fertile, and allow them to open their hearts to all who come to them.

Readings

Here follow some readings from some special sources that may be appropriate at the ceremony. This one is from a Hawaiian book that I found on the big island and presented to some friends at their wedding:

For the Power called God (Goddess) is both father and mother to all who seek it,
And apart from some physical feature there is no difference between man and woman as they incarnate.
They are molded from the same essence,
They are of the same mind,
They have the same degree of intelligence,
And both have access to the same spiritual source.
For the aim of all seekers is to purify the mind in order to reveal the spirit which is neither male nor female.[4]

Here is a Nahautl Indian love song:

I know not whether you have been absent:
I lie down with you, I rise up with you,
In my dreams you are with me.
If my eardrops tremble within my ears,
I know it is you moving within my heart.[5]

This is from Anne Morrow Lindbergh:

A good relationship has a pattern like a dance, and is built on the same rules. The partners do not need to hold on tightly, because they move confidently in the same pattern, intricate but swift, and free, like a country dance of Mozart's. To touch heavily would be to arrest the pattern and freeze the movement, to check the endlessly changing beauty of its unfolding. When you love someone you do not love that person all the time in exactly the same way, from moment to moment; that is an impossibility. And yet this is exactly what most of us demand. We have so little faith in the ebb and flow of life, of love, of relationships. We leap at the flow of the tide and resist in terror its ebb. We are afraid it will never return. We insist on permanence, on duration, on continuity, when the only continuity possible in life, as in love, is in growth, in fluidity, in freedom, in the sense that the dancers are free, barely touching as they pass, but partners in the same pattern.[6]

This is from Kahlil Gibran:

You were born together, and together you shall be forevermore. You shall be together when the white wings of death scatter your days. Aye, you shall be together even in the silent memory of God. (Goddess)
But let there be spaces in your togetherness, and let the winds of the heavens dance between you.
Love one another, but make not a bond of love: Let it rather be a moving sea between the shores of your souls. Fill each other's cup, but drink not from one cup. Give one another of your bread, but eat not from the same loaf.
Sing and dance together and be joyous, but let each one of you be alone, even as the strings of the lute are alone though they quiver with the same music.
Give your hearts, but not into each other's keeping, for only the hand of Life can contain your hearts.
And stand together, yet not too near together, for the pillars of the temple stand apart, and the oak tree and the cypress grow not in each other's shadow.[7]

Vows

Before the vows are exchanged, the person conducting the ceremony often says something to the group. Here is one simple example from a wedding I performed:

In the time I have known _____ and _____ , I have seen each of them begin walking the medicine path, the way of the ancient Grandmothers and Grandfathers. In so doing, they have deepened their commitment to each other and to all of us who know them and love them. For they have chosen to take us with them on their pilgrimage, their sacred marriage, in asking that we all be witnesses to their vows this day.

Here are the vows written by a couple whose ceremony I conducted. They wrote these vows themselves and then I read them back slowly while they repeated the words.

I, _____, take you, _____, in marriage
To be my life partner,
To walk, run, and dance this new path together,
To love, care and share,
To let the winds dance between us,
Let the fires burn within us,
And the waters flow through us,
On our sacred journey together.
With this ring may a new consciousness begin,
With this ring I thee wed,
With my hearts' faithful affections,
And my love to you, _____ .
Ho.

I, _____, am asking you, _____,
to join me as my life partner, once again,
as I travel on the sacred path
to higher consciousness.
I give to you from my heart,
my pledge of truthfulness,
commitment, and the freedom to soar
as high as the birds,
as we learn to love each other, love our family,
and love Gaia, the earth.
With this ring I give to you a reminder
of your strength and your vision,
as symbolized by the eagle.
I open to you my heart,
to give and to feel the great joy and happiness,
as we join together as husband and wife.

At the time of the vows, the gypsies do a blood bonding in which they take blood from the wrist of each of the partners and put it on a piece of cloth that is tied around the wrists of the couple. At pagan ceremonies, there is a similar custom known as handfasting. Each of the partners has a cord and the High Priestess blesses them with the elements. Then each of the partners takes an end and ties a knot in the cord while saying a blessing on their union. Next the High Priestess ties a knot in the center as she gives a blessing. If there are a small number of guests, each can tie a knot in the cord and give a blessing. If there are many guests, they can spontaneously give blessings without tying a knot. Then the hands of the couple are tied together with the knotted cord. While they are intertwined, all the guests visualize a sphere of white light around the couple as the High Priestess joins their auras. Music is played or a poem read while they stand and assimilate the energy. The cord is then removed and presented to the couple as a symbol of their union.[8]

Rings

The exchanging of the rings is a high point in the ceremony as significant as the vows. Often a special relative or friend (frequently a child) is selected as the ring bearer to hold the rings until the time is appropriate.

The person conducting the ceremony may talk briefly about the significance of rings. A ring forms a circle, with no beginning and no ending. The ring symbolizes the never ending nature of loving and giving; it also symbolizes the circle of life to which all belong—humans, animals, birds, insects. We are all one in the circle of life. This union also bonds these two individuals with that larger circle of life and love.

The couple may choose to talk about any important symbols they have put on their rings and share this with the group.

Then, as each of the partners places the ring on the other's finger, they may choose only to place it as far as the first knuckle, and have the other person place it the rest of the way to symbolize that each of the partners accepts the other's offer of marriage.

In some cases, couples choose other symbols, such as a crystal hung around each other's neck. In the wedding I mentioned earlier, the ring was made of cornmeal and was placed around the entire group, symbolizing the union of the couple not only with each other but with the community. It is the symbolism of the circle that is important and not the actual physical ring, though the physical object does provide a kind of bonding.

Pronouncement

After the rings are placed on each other's hands, the person conducting the ritual acts as a witness in pronouncing the couple married. Statements vary but are always short.

"In the name of the Goddess, these two beings, _____ and_____ are as one." (are bonded as one).

"In the spirit of the ancient ones, I witness your union as partners and bless you in the name of the Great Spirit."

In some traditions, a special ritual is then performed, as in the Jewish tradition where the man steps on a glass, symbolic of the shattering of the womb.

Songs and Dances

Musical and singing interludes should occur at various times in the ceremony. At the end of the ceremony some group singing and dancing is done as a celebration and expression of joy. Circle dances that join the entire group are fun, and some of the Sufi dances of universal peace may be used.

After singing and dancing, a bridge is sometimes formed by everyone at the wedding holding hands up in the air with a partner. The couple then go through this bridge and receive hugs and kisses and pinches as they make their way through to the other side. Pagans usually do a broom jump where the group sings and claps as the couple jump together over a broom which is placed horizontal a short distance from the ground.

Here is a good song for the group to sing at the end of a wedding ceremony:

(*Fantuzzi*)

You are my mother, you are my sister,
You are my lover, you are my friend,
You are the beginning, you are the center,
And you are beyond the end.

Chorus

I love you so, you help me to see,
To see you in all is to see you in me.
I'm in you and you're in me.
I'm in you and you're in me.

You are my father, you are my brother,
You are my lover, you are my friend,
You are the beginning, you are the center,
And you are beyond the end.

Chorus

The petals of the lotus, they are many,
But the flower is just one.
Philosophies, religions, they are many,
But the truth it is just one.

Chorus[9]

ENDNOTES

1. Niethammer, Carolyn, *Daughters of the Earth*, pp. 87–88.

2. Fox, Selena, *Planning and Performing a Pagan Wedding*, Circle Network News, Mt. Horbe, WI, 1989.

3. Shere, Jim, and Shere, Maria. *We Do* (work in progress).

4. Kealoha, Anna, *Songs of the Earth*, Celestial Arts, Berkeley, CA, 1989.

5. Bierhorst, John, ed., *In the Trail of the Wind: American Indian Poems and Ritual Orations*, Farrar, Straus & Giroux, NY, 1971.

6. Shere, Op. cit.

7. Shere, Op. cit.

8. Fox, Op. cit.

9. Kealoha, pp. 182–183.

Birth

We start as a fertilized egg in our mother's womb. In this safe enclosure we grow steadily over a nine-month period from a tiny fetus until the features of a fully grown living creature begin to form—legs and arms that kick against our mother's belly and sense organs that after birth will orient us to the phenomenal world.

There can be no more intense physical pain than the agony mothers undergo during labor and childbirth, and, as anyone who has ever watched a live birth knows, nothing can inspire more wonder than seeing a fully formed human being emerge from the mother's body. The great mystery, another "I" with consciousness of a separate existence is born. It is this knowledge of "I-ness" which separates human creatures from all other living beings and creates the question in every child's mind, "Where did I come from?"

Because of the length of time between conception and birth, it is thought that the connection between sexual intercourse and the growth of the fetus inside the woman was not fully understood in early times. However, since animals and other living creatures all have observable intercourse and different, but regular, periods of gestation, early peoples (as ancient artifacts indicate) soon discovered the connection between the man's fertilizing the female and the birth of a child. Perhaps in early societies the sense of "I-ness" was not as strong as it is now. Early people lived in small groups or in tribes; their commitment was to the community more than to any individual. A sense of individuality has grown with civilization. People always knew themselves to be other than crops or domesticated animals; slowly they developed personalities and a sense of self.

How does one understand the perception of coming from nothing and then losing one's identity in death? Many societies developed the belief that death would lead to some kind of afterlife; individuals were often buried with their personal articles. In Egypt an elaborate sense of life after death developed. If the person was important or wealthy enough, her/his body was wrapped for preservation; tombs were built for shelter; often servants were slain in order to be buried with their mistress or master, or figurines of servants were included in the tomb. The Pueblo Indians interred the bones of their family members in the mud walls of their apartment-like dwelling places with the idea that the dead would want to reside with the still living members of their family. In a later chapter we will discuss some medicine ways of dealing with dying

and death, but now we are at the dawn of life's story when the "I" of each of us first appears.

People in ancient societies, even with an awareness of how a child is conceived, didn't often have the means or understanding to control conception. Today, in sophisticated societies, exactly the opposite is true. Birth control devices are plentiful and easily obtained, while techniques to help the infertile and to prolong the years a woman is able to bear children are proliferating rapidly.

In the last thirty years, probably nothing in our society has changed more than our attitudes toward sexual activity and birth. Women have been given permission to enjoy sexual activity from their earliest years and often receive sensible and reliable advice on how to prevent unwanted pregnancies and protect themselves from disease. Unfortunately, as usual, this information is disseminated mainly among the upper and middle classes (and even among this favored group is often held back because of religious or other scruples) so that we have more teen-age pregnancies and single parent families in the United States now than ever before. Obviously, as in other realms of modern life, humanity's ability to manage its affairs has not caught up with its technical proficiency in tinkering with nature.

Also, in the last thirty years, openness toward differing birthing techniques has grown. Thirty years ago, if a woman could afford it, her child was born in a hospital. Usually she was given strong anesthesia to make the birth painless. Today women may still opt to have their babies in hospitals and to receive as many pain-killing drugs as the doctor deems advisable for the safety of the infant and mother. However, many women, with the help of a partner, participate in exercise classes to prepare for natural childbirth. More and more women are electing to have their babies in their own homes, delivered by a midwife rather than a doctor. And these practices are beginning to be sanctioned and encouraged by the medical establishment. Innovative birthing techniques are experimented with and enjoyed. Certain women want to deliver their babies in a pool of warm water so the infant will not suffer a sea change from the amniotic fluid to dry land. Others want to have the delivery witnessed by their partner, the midwife or doctor, and several friends and relatives. Many hospitals have a warm water environment ready for the newborn baby, along with soothing music. The baby is then given to the mother to "room-in" rather than begin life in the sterile environment of a plastic box in the newborn ward.

Where does this drama of birth begin? It begins with conception; it begins with the male sperm entering the female's vagina and fertilizing one small egg. Conception usually takes place when the female is fertile (we will discuss the various fertility cycles later), but in reality, it can happen anyplace, anywhere, and at any time of day. Far too often, conception is not intentional; it happens and then the mother has the choice to carry the seed and birth the child or abort. Intentional conception is good common sense. There is no need in our society for unwanted children—too many already exist. Since the woman is generally the person designated to care for the child after birth, as well as during pregnancy, it is difficult to overstress how important it is for a woman to conceive with intention. Intention means giving detailed thought to all the ramifications—emotional, physical, and material—which the birth of a child would entail.

In the last century men began to idealize women as "purer" than men, as befitted the "mothers of the race." An English medical textbook in 1857 stated flatly, "It is a *vile* aspersion to call women capable of sexual feeling."[1] Fortunately, today, women are acknowledged, even expected, to enjoy sexual pleasure—pleasure indeed seems the main purpose for engaging in sexual activity. Not so fortunately, as both women and men began to consider the woman's body primarily as an instrument of pleasure, women began to lose their sense of the sacredness of their own body and its unique and marvelous possibility of housing new life. A woman walking a medicine path is always conscious of her body as a source of life and her use of it is always intentional.

Conception—Conscious or Not?

It is possible, however, to go beyond intentional conception to conscious conception. Conscious conception is the result of both parents, both partners, female and male, knowing when it is proper to manifest a physical child through the ejaculation of semen into the vagina. This requires both partners being involved in a spiritual practice which allows them to have a sense and understanding of their higher purpose. Conscious conception involves calling in the being, connecting to the spirit of the child, before conceiving the

child physically. The implication here is that not only is a woman aware of her cycles in practicing natural birth control but she (with the help of her mate) can control physical conception through her spiritual being.

In order to practice conscious conception, the woman needs to be trained in meditation, creative visualization, yogic practices, or other spiritual disciplines. She may actively visualize herself conceiving a child; the egg within her womb being fertilized. Her partner can join her in this practice. She can establish a connection with her higher spiritual self, or any guide or teacher on the inner plane, to help her conceive a child that she (and her partner) are ready for psychologically and spiritually. Conscious conception must be practiced with a partner with whom you are completely in tune.

Another question that conscious conception raises today is the possibility of "in vitro fertilization." "In vitro fertilization" occurs when the male sperm is kept in a test tube and then injected into the female so that it fertilizes her ovum. This practice is available for women who have had difficulty conceiving as well as for lesbian women who want children. "In vitro fertilization" certainly involves planning and timing, though the process may seem too technological and mechanical for many. The whole question of "test tube babies" is a strongly controversial one, involving how we have changed the nature of conceiving children through "man-made" technology. Other practices now involve transplantation of fertilized eggs and embryos from the ovaries and wombs of women unable to conceive to other women, who then carry the embryos through the nine months, returning the child to the woman who supplied the egg. If the would-be mother is infertile, she can seek an egg donor whose egg will be fertilized "in vitro" by the male partner of the couple and then implanted into her womb so that she can have the full experience of carrying their child.

Conscious conception brings in the subject of conscious sex. Many women need to ask, "With whom am I lying and do I really want to conceive a child with this man?" Our present sexual lifestyle has eliminated this question from most women's minds. The use of birth control pills and intrauterine devices offer twenty-four-hour protection against conception. But it is time now to recognize that these methods of birth control rob us of consciousness; they anesthetize us to the deeper significance of the sexual union as well as making us totally unaware of our physical processes and cycles. To reclaim our true sexuality and power is to control our own bodies. Why give away that power to some chemical made in a laboratory or a mechanical device? To reclaim our power is also to experience the melding of individual egos with a higher source through the sexual act.

What Is Sex? What Are the Purposes of Sexual Intercourse?

Many cultures and religions would have us believe that the purpose of sex is solely for procreation. And in early societies this position made sense. Having enough people (often males) meant the difference between the survival and extinction of a tribe. In these cultures the sexual act became taboo, religiously prohibited, and sometimes seen as a "filthy" or "unclean" act when not for the purpose of conceiving children (that is, the woman was "unclean" and the man "unclean" in consorting with her). In certain parts of the world even today—in Africa, among African Muslims and others—young girls are subject to clitorectomy, the removal of the clitoris and severing the nerves of orgasm so that the girl can concentrate on her vagina as a reproductive vessel.[2] In Medieval times, women wore chastity belts, which were often locked by their husbands who kept the keys. All of this suggests that woman has some special bodily parts for creating children, but that these parts may not be used to give her any physical pleasure, emotional satisfaction, or spiritual and transcendent experiences. These practices also indicate that the husband, for reasons of property and possession, wished to be sure who the father of his wife's child was. "It's a wise child who knows its own father" refers ineluctably to the strong bodily connection between the mother and child not shared by the father. In addition, the male assumption of possessing the right to regulate the woman's sexuality perpetuates sexual anesthesia for women, as well as abuse, violence, and rape. In fact, the attitude toward sex in the Judeo-Christian tradition seems to come from a biased reading of the story of the Garden of Eden in Genesis. Eve's temptation to eat of the apple of *knowledge* is taken to downgrade woman (not the serpent) to the role of temptress. It reduces the meaning of "knowledge" to the knowledge of sexual congress rather than to possession of the same knowledge that God has of the world. Thus it is not the "apple" or "knowledge" that is forbidden fruit but the sexual gifts of women.

In total contrast to this view of sex is sex as a sacred practice, a relationship with all of life and nature. This view is found in Tantric teachings of India and Tibet, in Taoist sexual practices, and in many ritual sexual practices of Native American cultures and other tribal cultures throughout the world.

As Dolores La Chapelle points out in her book, *Sacred Land, Sacred Sex, Rapture of the Deep*, the basic creation story in Asia concerns a sister and brother carried in a hollow container, as a gourd, through a flood or other disaster. When the disaster is over, they realize they are the only humans left, and so they copulate and begin the human race.[3] The container or gourd symbolizes the "universal womb" or "Cosmic Mother." This story is in sharp contrast to the Old Testament one in which Eve, woman, is created from the rib of Adam, man. It also shows sex as a ritual act, not only creating humans again but bringing back the fertility of all nature.

In Asia, all energy comes out of the interaction of the *yin* and *yang*, which is constantly changing and flowing. Sexual energy therefore is a way to keep these in balance; it not only increases the energy between woman and man, but also between humans and nature.

The most important Taoist sexual ritual is called "Uniting the Chi's." This ritual occurred on either the new moon or full moon, after fasting. It began with a ritual dance and ended in either a public group ritual intercourse or in a succession of unions involving all those present, held in chambers along the sides of the temple courtyard.[4] Many of these public practices went underground and were performed in the Taoist temples due to Buddhist asceticism and the Confucian morals.

Chinese practices also control the timing of ejaculation through tightening certain muscles. This enables the semen to go back into the rest of the body and nourish those organs. There is also an acupuncture point, called the "tu-mo" point, which can be pressed so there is no ejaculation at orgasm. Those who practice these Taoist and Tantric exercises learn the location of this point and use it when they don't want to conceive.

In many tribal cultures, sexual ritual was used as a bonding with the spirit of the animals and nature. The

Utes performed a Bear Dance once a year in the spring. After setting up a cave of branches, the woman chose a man by plucking his sleeve (the female bear chooses her mate). The dance continued for three days, and from time to time a couple would leave the dance and go up into the hills to let out the spirit of the bear. A woman who plucked a man's sleeve might end up staying with him for just one night or for an entire hunting season or for many years.[5] This ritualized sex connected the tribe with their totem animal and prepared them for their hunting.

Attitudes toward sex are totally different in modern tribal societies; sex can be a way of showing affection, a bonding with spirits of animals, an emotional release, or a game. Some of the sexual rites of the Eskimos include playing ritual games like shutting out all light and then picking partners for sex. In tribal society, everyone is provided with sexual outlets, so there is no need to engage in sex surreptitiously or repress sexual energies.

Fertility Awareness

Most women are aware of their fertile cycles because they can feel ovulation taking place and see the mucus that appears at this time. However, women using birth control pills do not experience ovulation; the hormones in the pill inhibit ovulation. Many women are not in touch with their bodies enough to know that a change has taken place or are lucky enough not to feel any discomfort. Women using intrauterine devices often have difficulty determining their mucus cycles because the IUDs interfere with it.

The best way for a woman to become aware of her fertile cycle is to observe her mucus and start monitoring her sensations around the middle of her cycle so as to feel when she is ovulating. If this is difficult at first, a thermometer can be used to check the temperature. Temperature usually rises during ovulation and then begins to drop after a few days. Checking out mucus with a speculum (mirror) is also helpful; you can see the difference in the mucus during ovulation, when it is wet, sticky, and slippery. An excellent book to guide women through this process is *The Natural Birth Control Book* by Art Rosenblum, published by the Aquarian Research Foundation, Philadelphia, PA. The book is usually up-dated every few years. The revised *Our Bodies, Our Selves* is a useful guide to any kind of gynecological self-examination.

There is also another fertility cycle based on the relationship between the sun and moon in the astrological horoscope. The distance between the sun and moon determines the maximum fertility time. When the sun and moon return to this same angular distance a woman is fertile. (For example a woman born at first quarter moon would be fertile every month at the first quarter.) Three and one-half days are taken before this exact time and one-half day afterwards. That makes a time period of four days *in addition* to the ovulation cycle (unless they overlap). *The Natural Birth Control Book* also has tables in the back for determining the sun/moon angle and for each month to see when that angle occurs. A common sense way to discover if your own body conforms to your astrological map is to combine watching for ovulation through temperature and mucus checks and coordinating these with your astrological fertility period.

Infertility

For many women, the problem is not to prevent pregnancy, but to become pregnant. In order to conceive a child women have often undergone painful or humiliating procedures such as the blowing open of their fallopian tubes and frequent examinations of the uterus. Often nothing is found to be wrong, and the doctor may then recommend fertility drugs, which influence the body in an unnatural way (multiple births are common with fertility drugs).

In my work as a healer and medical astrologer, I have seen many women with this problem. Sometimes it can be helped through dietary changes, nutritional supplements, and certain herbs. More often there is the need to do some deeper psychological and spiritual work. What are one's fears in bringing in a child? There may be unresolved conflicts with one's own mother and a wish to not repeat those patterns. Often there are fears that one's mate would not stay around and help support the child. Possibly there are deeper issues stemming from other lifetimes where a child died or became ill. Or there may be particular things to work out with the individual soul coming in, so there is resistance and consequently the inability to conceive. Many times there is the need to understand one's "dharma." Is it in one's plan to have one's own children or to use one's mothering energy for others, as in the case of certain healers, nurses, doctors, midwives? Too much time spent with her own children might take the healer from people who need her energy. This is an issue on which each couple must be clear before considering the possibility of conceiving.

Practices for Conceiving Consciously

Conceiving a child is a sacred function. In many tribal societies, as well as in ancient cultures, there were special practices and rituals for conception. Both the Pythagoreans and the Essenes performed rituals to prepare the way on earth for an incoming soul.[6]

Many spiritual and metaphysical writings suggest that the parents follow a spiritual path and lifestyle to prepare themselves as vehicles for a particular type of soul.

Native Americans perform extensive rituals for calling in a child. The following was shared with me by Oh Shinnah Fastwolf.

Both parents fast for four days and go to the top of a mountain. There they pay attention to their dreams and any messages they are given concerning the being who will be coming to them. They dig a hole and plant a crystal in it. The father sucks on the woman's navel, then calls to the spirit of the being. The father often sings a song to the spirit. Sometimes they make a medicine wheel with pollen for this spirit they are attracting.

The navel is often referred to as the "energy womb"; in occult literature it is symbolized as a flower opening up to invite the soul to make contact with its new home.

If the parents are not able to spend the four days fasting, they can still perform a ceremony to bring in the spirit of their child. They can visualize a thread of light connecting this being to theirs; this thread of light becomes the umbilical cord.[7] They can meditate on the best ways to allow the being to come through and prepare themselves inwardly to receive the new spirit.

If more parents communicated with the spirits of the children before bringing them into physical incarnation, parent-child bonding might be easier. Relationships could be more harmonious, and perhaps there would be less abuse, physical and verbal, between parents and children.

Abortion

Performing abortions in a spiritual way, a way that allows the being to understand what is going on, is extremely important. Oh Shinnah relates that the mother can plant three beans after she finds out she is pregnant. If one bean comes up, she can do anything she wants, birth the child or abort it. If two beans come up, she is allowed to communicate with the child so that it will leave her womb. She can use herbs to help with this. She can tell the child to come back at another time or go to another sister. If three beans come up, then she must have the child.

If a woman chooses to abort a child, she must do a ceremony to release it. It is preferable to do this with both parents if possible.

Here is a ceremony that is done in certain Native American tribes:

The ceremony is done at sunrise out on the land. The mother and father face the direction they associate with this being. They call out the name of the being three times, or some spirit name. The mother holds a star rock or small crystal in her right hand; she breathes her prayers into this crystal. Then she talks to the spirit, swings her body three times counterclockwise, and, with a yell of release, throws the star rock or crystal onto the land. (Cornmeal or tobacco can also be used.)

Wherever an abortion is done, even if it is done in a hospital or doctor's office, it can always be performed as a spiritual ceremony. One can always take a medicine bag, a crystal, do some prayers, and talk to the spirit of the child to explain what is going on.

Herbs for Abortion

If a woman is going to use herbs to abort, she needs to be careful which herbs she uses, and she needs to be aware that herbs are only the catalyst to help the body. The real work is the release of the spirit that must be done on the inner planes, through speaking with the being, meditation, and ritual. That is why herbs work well for some women and not for others. There is also the fear factor to consider when a woman drinks the herbal teas—How long will it take? Will I bleed too much? Will this really work?

She must have confidence in her body and faith that this is a simple process and something she can do herself. If a woman is confident, then she can go ahead and use the following herbal formula, which is the simplest one I know (and very effective).

To 2 cups of water, add 2 teaspoons pennyroyal and 2 teaspoons blue cohosh. Simmer this mixture for 10–15 minutes and drink about 4 cups a day for three days. **Do not drink more than this amount.**

It is also helpful to take certain vitamin and mineral supplements such as B complex, particularly B-6, magnesium and manganese for the hormonal changes. These should be taken several times a day. Keep the diet light, lots of green, leafy vegetables, some grains, light proteins, not much fruit or sweet foods, to prevent getting "spaced out." The grains and vegetables will keep the body alkaline, which is beneficial.

Pregnancy

During the nine months of pregnancy, a woman is given a chance to bond with the child she is carrying. This bonding while the child is in the womb is very important; the activities the mother is involved in during this time obviously influence the being she is carrying.

It is important for her to slow down, both in a physical and mental sense. Increased meditation, increased creative activities will expand her intuitive awareness and help her keep centered. All these things are necessary as she prepares for her labor and the birthing. Physical exercises and prenatal yoga are also essential to keep her body balanced and her muscles flexible.

Certain herbs and nutritional supplements are important as she undergoes the various hormonal changes and nourishes the fetus within.

The following herbs are important drunk as teas.

Raspberry leaf	Good source of magnesium and known to strengthen abdominal muscles.
Comfrey	Good source of calcium and keeps all mucosal linings lubricated.
Squawvine	Excellent herb, often mixed with raspberry leaf to prepare the uterus for childbirth.
Nettle leaves	Good source of iron.

For morning sickness, some of the nervine herbs such as chamomile, hops, and spearmint may be used. A good mixture is the following:

Meadowsweet	*2 parts*
Black horehound	*2 parts*
Camomile	*2 parts*[8]

Nutritional supplements include a good multivitamin mineral, bioflavonoids, zinc, calcium/magnesium/potassium supplement, and in some cases B complex, free form amino acid capsules, and a liquid iron supplement.

Foods high in iron as beets; the sea vegetable, dulse; red cabbage; blackstrap molasses; cherries; prunes; cherry and prune juice should be included in the diet. Also lots of green, leafy vegetables high in mineral content provide calcium, magnesium, potassium, and trace minerals—all important in the diet.

During pregnancy, there should be an emphasis on activities that are inner directed, allowing the mother to communicate and bond with her child. Creative activities, such as writing, beading, sewing, painting, listening to or making music, and crafts serve to heighten a mother's intuitive function. Sharing these activities with her partner can also be enriching; making articles such as blankets, clothes, moccasins and a medicine bag for the baby is a good way to connect with the spirit of the child.

Blessingway Ceremony

The Navajos have a Blessingway ceremony for birth that can be used to honor the mother. It is usually done about one or two months before the expected birth on the new moon or full moon or other appropriate time for a ceremony. The Blessingway is usually done with women, although the men can have a ceremony at a separate place honoring the father, and both can come together later to share food and songs.

A special altar is built in the middle of the circle. On this altar are articles that symbolize fertility and reproduction such as statues of fertility goddesses, flowers, very ripe round fruits, shells from the sea, eggs (the egg was one of the earliest symbols of fertility and the goddess), and beautiful crystals. Gifts that are brought for the mother and the baby may be placed in the center or close by.

A special place of honor is created for the mother-to-be in the circle. Then everyone is smudged with cedar or sage and the ceremony is begun. The leader may ask four special women beforehand to represent the four directions. They call in and make prayers to the directions, each lighting a candle as she does so. The Goddess in her various forms may also be called in.

After the four directions and the Goddess are called, the women form a birth canal with a pair of women forming an arch. As each woman passes through the arch, she is kissed by each of the two women and then she forms an arch with the next woman, until all the women are in this formation. The mother-to-be goes through last. While the women are passing through this canal, the chant, "By a woman you were born into this circle, by a woman you were born into this world" is sung. Sometimes the birth canal is done before calling in the directions, but I prefer to do it afterwards.

Next the midwife, if she is present, washes the feet of the prospective mother. This symbolizes that the midwife is her servant and helper. While this is being done, another woman, preferably the mother, brushes and rearranges the woman's hair in a new way, which is symbolic of the changes she will encounter in motherhood. She then bathes and massages the feet of the mother-to-be. The foot bath contains many herbs and flowers that are sweet smelling and nurturing.

Now it is time for the sharing—when each woman presents a gift and makes a blessing. At one of the Blessingways I attended, each woman was asked to bring a bead for a necklace to be made for the baby. As she presented this bead, she told where it came from and why it was special for the baby. All the beads were then placed on the altar. Prayers were made with the beads and also other sharings, poems and songs, when women presented the mother with gifts for herself and for the new baby. This is a special time to honor the mother and she is often presented with clothes to wear for the birthing, oils to place on her skin, special objects for the birthing altar.

After the presentation of gifts, the midwife or another woman who is leading the ceremony, takes out some wool and each woman ties some around her hand so she will be connected to the mother and know when she is giving birth. This wool should not be cut until after the baby is born; it serves as an important thread to connect the sisters to the mother. When all this is done, there may be more chanting and perhaps drumming or other music along with sharing of food. Here are a few special songs for the Blessingway:

We All Came to Welcome You

We all came to welcome you,
We all came to your birth.
We all came to welcome you,
To welcome you to earth.

And I was there to love you,
I was there to love you
And give my body for
Your quick and easy entrance,
Here through heaven's door.

Grandmother Song

(*I wrote this for a friend shortly before the birth of her baby.*)

The Grandmothers they are coming,
They're coming to this Earth,
They're coming for the Healing,
They're coming for the Birth.

They're bringing herbs and feathers,
Pollen, tobacco too,
They're carrying giant crystals,
And cornmeal that is blue.

The Grandmothers they are coming,
They're coming to this Earth,
They're coming for the Healing,
They're coming for the Birth.

Labor and Birth

Some of the information on birthing that is presented here comes from various Native American traditions and has been shared with me by one of my medicine teachers, Oh Shinnah Fastwolf.

Before the birth, the parents need to find a birthing feather. They can make prayers with tobacco to guide them to the correct feather. Blue heron is known to be the best but other bird feathers would also be okay (except owl or buzzard). A string is tied on the feather and it is looped over the branch of a tree. If it's still there in the morning, then it is the right feather.

The parents also need to get a birthing crystal which will be used during labor. Eight other crystals should be obtained which will be placed around the mother's bed (one in each of the eight directions).

Often these crystals become giveaways to the midwife and anyone else assisting at the birth.

When the mother begins labor and calls her family members and friends to assist, the house should be smudged with cedar or sage. Anyone who comes in later or who comes to see the baby should also be smudged. The friends who are there should also build an altar in another part of the house besides the birthing altar. This is a place where they can focus their prayers while the mother is in labor. It can have a fertility goddess on it, special crystals, feathers, and herbs that will help the mother. The mother and her partner also build a birthing altar near the bed or place where she will give birth. On this are any special objects that have been presented to the baby before-hand, as a medicine bag or moccasins, feathers, crystals, candles, and family empowerment objects as a special medicine staff or rattle or prayer arrow.

During labor, a tea of raspberry leaves and squawvine is helpful. If an herb is needed to stimulate the uterus into contraction, the best one is golden seal.[9] It can be drunk as a tea by infusing the powder for 10–15 minutes or if this is undesirable, it can be taken in capsules.

The mother should be in a comfortable place where she can focus on her breathing. The father or partner can work with the mother, helping her to breathe rhythmically through maintaining eye contact. The partner also brings the feather down over the belly to help the contractions and uses the crystal to help bring the baby down, by moving the crystal over the solar plexus.

When the baby comes out, a song may be sung by the mother or both parents as the mother holds the baby on her breast. The first thing the baby hears is the mother's heart beat and this special song. The cord is cut by a relative, usually the grandmother, who holds the crystal where it is to be cut. Pollen is put on the mother's palms, solar plexus, crown chakra, and tip of her tongue. Pollen is also placed on the baby's palms, soles of feet, crown chakra, solar plexus, and tip of tongue.

The father or partner goes out and calls to the power of the four directions. He (or she) calls out the child's name to the directions and when he (or she) comes back the name is whispered in the child's ear.

The cord is dried and put in the baby's medicine bag. The placenta is frozen or dried and then planted under a tree that becomes the baby's tree. Before the placenta is frozen, a small piece is cut off. Either this is cooked for the mother to eat or a small piece is dried in a slow oven and it is pulverized and placed in capsules. The placenta contains much nutritional value that helps the mother regain her strength and energy. It is used in Chinese medicine for healing many conditions. The cord from the placenta is also dried and it is used as a teething ring.

In the Navajo tradition, a woman usually gave birth inside the hogan. A red handwoven belt was suspended from the roof beam so that she could grip it. A knot was tied near the lower end, and corn pollen placed along the belt. Corn pollen was also placed on the woman's body, in her mouth, on her head, and down her body. The singer or medicine person helping at the birth brought a brush made of eagle, owl, and other feathers, including a crow's feather. He (Mostly this was a male, since Navajo women cannot conduct sings unless they have completed menopause. The prejudice against the sexually fertile woman seems to crop up in most societies, tribal or individualistic.) moves the brush around her while she is kneeling in labor. The brush is moved downward and a song, known as the "baby-move song" is sung. An unraveling ceremony is also done, often with the woman's hair string, and is symbolic of freeing the baby. Then her husband or another female relative grasps her from behind and winds their arms around her waist and bears down on her to assist the pain and to help the baby to move.[10]

Herbs for Nursing

Herbs that are helpful for milk production are goat's rue, aniseed, blessed thistle, caraway seeds, fennel seeds, fenugreek seeds, and vervain. Goat's rue is the most powerful and can be drunk three times a day if necessary.[11] These seeds are rich in volatile oils and can be combined to make a tea:

Caraway	2 parts
Fennel	1 part
Aniseed	1 part
or	
Fenugreek	2 parts
Aniseed	1 part

To make these teas, crush 2 tablespoons of the seeds and put them in cold water. Simmer them and then remove from the heat. Let them stand for 10 minutes, covered to reduce the loss of volatile oils. Drink a cup three times a day.

If the milk flow needs to be stopped, the most effective herb is red sage, or just ordinary garden sage, made into an infusion and drunk three times daily.[12]

Naming Ceremonies

It is important to hold a ceremony when the baby is formally named and presented to the community or friends. The naming ceremony (similar to Christening) is often done on a special day, such as a new moon or other significant time in terms of the astrological or cosmic forces and the relationship they have to the baby's birth horoscope. For example, a baby whose birth I attended will be named three months after she was born, on a new moon that is conjunct (aligned with) the planet Venus, as in her natal horoscope, she has the planet Venus right near the Ascendant.

Oh Shinnah has shared that at the naming ceremony it is appropriate to pick a special tree which will be the baby's tree and under which the placenta and the umbilical cord (which has been frozen or dried) will be buried. This tree represents the Tree of Life; oak, poplar, elm, willow, alder, or any other tree may be chosen. It is good for the relatives and friends present to form a circle around this tree and chant. Often there is a bowl of water at the foot of the tree and some cornmeal, (many of the Wiccan ceremonies use barley or corn as well as a bowl of salt, and a garlic bulb).[13] The parents may choose a guardian for the child (similar to the concept of godmother) or elder or grandmother who will participate in the ritual with them.

The guardian or elder offers prayers for the baby. The mother places the baby by the tree and one woman in the circle takes the cornmeal and pours it on the earth, offering a prayer to Earth Mother for the baby to be protected by Earth Mother and always have enough food. Another woman or man takes the bowl of water and prays for the child's life force to be strong and emotions to be clear. Sky Father may be asked to bless the child. Individuals may then offer their prayers for the baby, at which time they may put something in the baby's medicine bag. Afterwards, the cornmeal and water remaining, along with the salt and garlic bulb if they are used, are buried with the placenta and the umbilical cord under the baby's tree. Then the baby's name is spoken aloud, often chanted by the father or mother to the four directions. The baby's secret or spiritual name is also chanted by the elder or guardian. Everyone then chants and drums and celebrates the naming. Later there is often dancing and feasting.

Examples of Native American Ceremonies

According to some Native American traditions, eight days after the baby is born it is taken to the morning circle for prayers. A medicine wheel is made for the baby and special objects are placed in the baby's medicine bundle. The Zuni present the infant to the sun at this time. First the head is washed by the aunts, the women of the father's clan, then cornmeal is placed in the baby's hand, and the infant is taken outdoors, facing the east, at the moment of sunrise. Cornmeal is sprinkled to the rising sun and a prayer is spoken by the paternal grandmother.

The Omaha had an interesting ceremony when the child was ready to walk. The child needed a new pair of moccasins for this ceremony. After the ceremony, the child's baby name was thrown away. In the tent where the ceremony was held, a fire burned in the center. To the east was a stone upon which the child's feet would be placed. This stone was symbolic of long life. The mother brought the child to the tent and approached the medicine person who represented the thunder. She asked that the child wear moccasins at this time. The child entered the tent carrying his new moccasins. The medicine person directed a chant to the winds and the child was then turned upon the stone.

Turned by the winds goes the one I send yonder;
Yonder he goes who is whirled by the winds;
Goes, where the four hills of life and the four winds are standing;
There in the midst of the winds do I send him,
Into the midst of the winds, standing there.[14]

Among the Mandan tribe, until the child received a name, it was not considered a part of the village but of the "baby home" from which it had come. When the child received a name her/his status in the tribe was recognized. The Mandan believed that there was a baby hill, like an earth lodge, in which an old man cared for them. If a child died before being named, it returned to the baby hill. If a woman was childless, she would go to one of these hills and pray for a child.[15]

ENDNOTES

1. Taylor, G. Rattray, *Sex in History*, Vol. VI, Thames & Hudson, 1953.

2. Sjoo, Monica, and Mor, Barbara, *The Great Cosmic Mother*, p. 5.

3. La Chapelle, Dolores, *Sacred Land, Sacred Sex, Rapture of the Deep*, p. 261.

4. *Ibid.*

5. *Ibid.*, p. 260.

6. Schultz, Karen, "The Conception Mysteries," in *Conscious Conception*, Baker, Baker & Slayton, p. 285.

7. *Ibid.*, p. 286.

8. Hoffmann, David, *The Holistic Herbal*, p. 103.

9. Hoffmann, p. 103.

10. Bailey, Flora, "Same Sex Beliefs and Practices in Navajo Country," *Papers of Peabody Museum*, Cambridge, MA, Vol. 40:2, 1980.

11. Hoffmann, p. 103.

12. *Ibid.*

13. Budapest, Z., *The Holy Book of Women's Mysteries, Part II*, p. 57.

14. Fletcher, Alice, and LaFlesche, Francis, *The Omaha*, p. 119.

15. Bowers, Alfred, *Mandan Social and Ceremonial Organization*, p. 60.

Menopause

In women's medicine, one of the most powerful times of life is menopause; it marks a passage to Grandmother energy, to the wise woman or crone phase. It is the time in Native American tradition when one can become a Medicine Woman or shaman.

The words *crone* and *witch* hold many negative connotations as a result of the Inquisition in Europe and the burning of so many of the wise women. The English word *crone* derives from the Old French *kronje*, which was an old ewe or hag, also from the French word *carogne*, "carrion." In German, *krone* means "crown." Webster's dictionary defines *crone* as a "withered old woman." In fact, the crone was the designation of the third of the Triple Goddess' three aspects and represented old age, death, winter, the waning moon. The crone represented the third, postmenopausal phase of women's lives; it was believed that women became very wise when they no longer shed the lunar "wise blood" but kept it inside.[1] The crone also had a fearsome, destructive side as witnessed in some of the crone goddesses—Hecate, Kali, Ereshkigal, Cerridwyn, Hel, Morgan.

The word *witch* according to Skeat's Etymological Dictionary derives from medieval English *wicche*, formerly Anglo-Saxon *wicca* (m.) or *wicce* (f.), which was a corruption of *witga*, "a seer or diviner" from Anglo-Saxon *witan*, "to see" or "to know." The words *wit* and *wisdom* come from the same roots.[2] Early Medieval England had female clan leaders who exercised matriarchal rights in lawgiving and law enforcement; the Magna Carta of Chester called them *judices de wich*, "judges who were witches."[3] Female elders once had political power among the clans, but patriarchal religion and law gradually took it away from them and called them witches in order to dispose of them.[4]

Because older women hold so much power, they have been revered as well as feared throughout the centuries. In the Iroquois Five Nations, women chose the *sachem* or chief and also decided if the men they selected were doing a good job. Each clan was divided into lineages, and at the head of each lineage was an older woman, the matron, who derived her position from her age and her qualities of leadership and diplomacy. She coordinated the economic activities of the female clan members; when one of the sachems died, the matron of his lineage, in council with her female relatives, selected his successor.[5]

Among the Cherokees in southeastern United States, the women voted with the men in selecting leaders. In addition, the women in each Cherokee town elected delegates to the Women's Council, which was presided over by the "Beloved Woman." This matriarch and her council challenged the authority of the chiefs when they thought the welfare of the tribe was in jeopardy.[6] Women also had much power among the Sinkaietk, a Salish tribe along the Columbia River in Washington. A woman who was related to the chief often served as chieftess of the tribe. If the chieftess' decision differed from the chief, the people were free to follow either.[7]

In northern California, the Nisenan sometimes had a woman at their head. The chieftainship was primarily hereditary and, if on the death of a chief, there was no male relative competent to fill the position, the deceased's widow, daughter, or niece might be chosen. Her measure of strength depended on the degree of support she had from the people.[8] In the Pueblo societies in the Southwest, men ran the government and controlled the ceremonies, but women had an important place in religion and since they controlled the households, they had more say in civil matters.[9] Among the Hopi, the leader of each Hopi town was assisted by a woman relative who was called "Keeper of the Fire." She was chosen for this honor on the basis of her wisdom, intelligence, and interest in religious ceremony. The male chief kept his office in this woman's home and consulted her on many decisions. Every clan in the Hopi village was also headed by a matriarch, or clan mother, who had certain privileges as a result of her seniority. The clan mother was consulted by her male relatives on matters which fell within her realm of competence.[10]

The western Apache recognized some of the stronger and more influential women as "women chiefs." These women were often wives of chiefs or subchiefs. They gained their status because they displayed wisdom and strength and were an example of Apache womanhood. They organized other women in gathering food and gave advice on child care and family living.[11]

In the Seneca tradition, (The Seneca are one of the five tribes of the Iroquois Five Nations and are based in upstate New York.) when a woman begins her changes, she counsels with the grandmothers of the tribe and chooses a particular subject on which to focus in preparation for teaching the spirituality of that subject. Possible subjects might be the spirituality of dreams, of animals, of trees, of food, of children and women. At the end of a year of changes, the woman was accepted as a Grandmother and had the opportunity to represent her clan at the Elders Council. The clan mothers determined the family structure and conducted the pipe ceremonies at moon lodges. After completing menopause, the women also selected the chiefs.[12]

In pre-Christian Europe, as well as in the Middle East and Egypt, elder women also held positions of power and responsibility. They were healers and midwives, conducting ceremonies for all events from birth through death. As scribes, they set up calendars for religious observances, transcribed scriptures, and administered libraries.[13] They also conducted rituals at many temples of the Goddess. With the rise of Christianity and patriarchal society, these High Priestesses and Medicine Women became dishonored, banished from their homes, tortured, and murdered. This treatment of healers, herbalists, and all those who practiced any earth-based religion continued from the twelfth to the nineteenth centuries.

Prior to this time women held positions of authority and power. Just as the councils of Native American Grandmothers chose the sachems or chiefs, so was it the custom among the Picts, Gaels, Teutons, Celts, Galatians, Lydians, Scythians, Sumerians, Akkadians, and others for councils of elder women to choose the kings and war leaders.[14] Most of these early European and Middle-Eastern cultures traced descent through the mother. Most scholars agree that Crete was in fact, a matriarchy, a theocracy ruled by a High Priestess.[15]

What happened then to the older woman to cause her to lose her power? And how has she begun to regain this power?

The witch hunts during the Inquisition and the subsequent denigration of "witches," "crones," and "hags" as old, feeble, useless, and even evil has been challenged and changed with the reappearance of the Goddess religion. In prehistory the older women were the originators of the law. The Greeks and Romans attributed the foundations of their law to the ancestral Mother Goddess, Demeter or Ceres.[16] In Egypt, the name of one of the oldest goddesses, Heqit or Hekat, was formed from the root, *heq*, "intelligence," which also designated a tribal ruler in the predynastic period.[17] The Greeks called this deity Hecate and made her the crone form of the Mother of the Gods. (She was later made Queen of the Witches in Christian times.) The Egyptians traced their descent through mothers and regarded women as founders of families.[18] Elder women made the rules for the families and their codices, attributed to the *heq* of tribal mothers, became the laws of Maa or Maat (meaning the Mother of Truth).[19]

The word *hag* used to mean a "holy one" from Greek *hagia*, as in *hagiolatry*, "worship of saints." It may also have been related to the Egyptian *heq*. During the Middle Ages, when women practiced the "fairy religion," "hag" was said to mean the same as "fairy."[20]

There is a spiritual and metaphysical explanation for what happened during this period in European history when women were punished and burned at the stake: the Goddess was in hiding. The Goddess was in her "dark moon" phase just as the moon goes through its "dark phase" each month. She gradually emerged and manifested herself in the feminist movement, gaining more and more strength politically and spiritually. As Gaia, the Earth Mother, she was recognized by many ecologically minded scientists after the birthing of the Gaia hypothesis. With this reemergence of the Goddess, the role of older women and the honor and respect due them has returned.

Qualities of the Crone or Grandmother

The first quality we associate with Grandmother energy or croneship is wisdom. Older women are the keepers of the wisdom and traditions in their families, clans, tribes, covens, and communities. The primary wisdom or knowledge that the Grandmothers have is the understanding of the two greatest mysteries—birth and death. It was the patriarchy's fears of this knowledge—the herbs, the midwifery practices, the communication with those who had departed—that led to the denigration of the wise woman. The mystery associated with older women and birth is exemplified by two biblical stories where older women conceived. One is Sarah in the Old Testament (Genesis 17:17), who bore her child at the age of ninety. The other is in the New Testament (Luke 1:36); Elizabeth, mother of John the Baptist, was also postmenopausal when she bore John. This happens, on occasion, to women who have stopped their bleeding and suddenly find themselves pregnant. What greater mystery than this? Both of the biblical stories, of course, are also symbolic of the wisdom that these women, Sarah and Elizabeth, gave birth to.

Another quality of the Crone/Grandmother is the ability to go between two worlds; this is the shape shifting shamanistic talent that enables the wise woman to go "beyond the veil," particularly at the time of All Hallows. It was claimed that European witches held ceremonies in graveyards as did the Oriental dakinis. Devotees of Kali gathered at night in the atmosphere of cremation grounds to familiarize themselves with the sights and smells of death in order to overcome their fears.[21]

When a woman leaves the mothering phase and enters Grandmother consciousness, she takes on a new sense of freedom. Mothering, whether it be one's physical children, clients or friends, requires a lot of close attention and dedication of large amounts of energy. Grandmothering, however, is different in that the grandmother's arms are wider (more wisdom), but farther away. She has paid her dues, so to speak, given her time as mother, healer, therapist, counselor. And though she may continue to do so, she does it in a different way—with more detachment, with more freedom for herself.

As a result of this freedom, there is a lot of creativity unleashed in this phase of life. One's responsibilities and duties on the earth plane have lifted and it is time to express this freedom in art, poetry, song, dance, and crafts. It is a joyous time, a time for celebration and expression. The creative urges that were put into mothering and caretaking have been freed up and many new doors are open. So many women pursue the arts after retiring and after their families have grown. The list of well known and accomplished writers, musicians, dancers, painters, and craftswomen is usually comprised primarily of older women. A woman I know spent a lifetime as a doctor in a small town in Maine. She was always on-call and utilized folk medicine and herbs as well as acupuncture techniques. When she turned sixty-five, she retired and enrolled in the university as an art student, something she had always wanted to do. Now she is painting large canvasses and enjoying expressing herself artistically.

With this artistic freedom, comes a sense of wildness and release. All those things which were prohibited earlier seem possible now. One woman shared with me that she no longer had to dress a certain way to please her boss, or to attract men; she finally realized that she could dress to please herself, to express her own being and individuality. Sexual freedom is an-other strong experience of older women. Often bound up in marriages that were inhibiting for much of their lives, they are now able to get in touch with their deeply passionate natures. For some women this means divorce and new relationships; for others it may mean having relationships with other women or becoming bi-sexual. Older women are closer to the androgynous state (balance of female and male energy) and therefore can enjoy relationships in a new way. Relationship now is based more on sharing and mutual interests; less on need and dependency.

The wisdom, freedom, wildness, and self-expression can only lead to a sense of power. Power results from being true to one's self and one's own particular dharma. Power to stand up to authority figures and assert one's own worth as a woman and as an individual. Power to pursue any avenues in life, even where doors seemed closed before. Power to make boundaries and *say no* when one has to.

Power to *be and exist*, which is to tap into the universal energy, the Great Mystery, and to know that one is truly a part of this larger cosmic support system. This, perhaps, is the core meaning of Grandmother consciousness and crone wisdom.

Responsibilities of the Crone/ Grandmother

The first responsibility of this phase of womanhood is to nurture oneself. Only by nurturing oneself can one nurture others, and, in turn, Mother Earth. Nurturing means attending to all one's needs, physical as well as emotional and spiritual. It means eating good, clean, nutritious food; it means exercising one's body, having massage and other relaxing treatments; it means seeking relationships that are supportive; it means being involved in activities that are mentally satisfying and stimulating.

When a woman is nurtured herself, then she can attend to others and the needs of the great mother, the Earth Mother. Then she can use her wisdom to support change and growth in her sisters and brothers, to attune others to the plight of the planet.

As a source of wisdom, the Crone/Grandmother can help younger women to understand their role; to balance their bodies; to instruct them on the purposes and functions of relationship, motherhood, and on their duties to their community or tribe. The Grandmother can help other beings to cross over to the next world by imparting her wisdom, her love, and her knowledge of the Great Mystery.

Perhaps, most important of all, she bears the responsibility to be beautiful—physically, emotionally, spiritually. It is the Grandmother who represents the Great Earth Mother, the Goddess; she needs to portray Her with every step she takes, with every thought she thinks, with every action she makes. The Navajo say "Walk in Beauty" and this is truly the key to Grandmother energy.

Becoming a Medicine Woman

In Native American tradition, a woman does not become a Medicine Woman until she has completed her bleeding cycle, until the mothering phase is truly over. It is then that she has the time to heal and nurture others outside of her family. She may have spent her younger years learning the various forms of medicine—the plants and the herbs, the ways of setting bones, the chants and ceremonies involved in healing, the way of the sweat lodge, shamanic healing and journeying to other worlds (not every Medicine Woman uses shamanic techniques). But it is only after the time of her menopause that she is considered to have the wisdom and compassion to begin doctoring.

In the Seneca tradition, it is never spoken which members of the tribe are medicine people. One does not call oneself a medicine person, though others may say it of a person. There are five requirements for a Seneca medicine person. The person first must be a counselor who can assist others in finding their personal talents and life path. The counselor works with the Medicine Wheel and tribal law and wisdom. The second requirement is that the person must be a historian of earth records and understand the first four worlds as well as the prophecies for the future worlds. Third, the person must be an herbalist and healer and be able to diagnose illnesses of the body, mind, and spirit. Fourth, she must be a seer and be able to contact the spirit world and interpret signs and symbols. The fifth requirement is the ability to teach all aspects of the wisdom to others.[22]

Physiological Considerations

During the menopausal years, many changes take place within the body. There is no reason why these changes should cause any distressing symptoms if the body is kept balanced with good foods, nutritional supplements, herbs, and plenty of exercise. In my own life, I had a four-year cycle where menstrual periods were irregular before stopping completely, but I never experienced any "hot flashes" or discomfort. This is true of many of my friends and clients as well.

One of the prime factors in approaching the physiology of menopause is to consider this phase as the truly natural cycle it is. That may mean for many women letting go of old programs, fears, and information that the medical establishment and many books (even some written by feminists) put forth. In fact, it is not necessary to have estrogen replacement therapy (ERT) or a hysterectomy no matter how extreme one's symptoms may be.

Women go through similar changes at puberty and with the correct nutrients, the body adapts to these new hormone levels. Basically, the hormone estrogen decreases after the child-bearing years. When it reaches a level too low to maintain the menstrual cycle, menopause begins. During this time, the ovaries stop producing the monthly egg and stop secreting the monthly estrogen.

Often women have physiological symptoms as "hot flashes," depression, and irritability. The cause of hot flashes has never been completely explained. Theories are that it is caused by irregular levels of estrogen and progesterone in the blood stream or irregular levels of another hormone called follicle stimulating hormone (FSH).[23]

My own experience in working with women is that the ones who get the hot flashes are those whose bodies are out of balance, usually those who are eating "fast foods" and sugar, drinking coffee, and smoking cigarettes. Women who tend to low blood sugar and have had problems with PMS often get hot flashes. When important minerals are added to the body, the blood sugar levels become normal, and the hot flashes are alleviated. A better term for "hot flashes" might be "power surges," because they certainly enable women to experience their heat. Some women even get used to them and rather enjoy them.

The ability to nurture and care for one's own body is an important issue here. If one is committed to nurturing oneself and keeping one's body beautiful and in balance, the physiological transition is easy.

Treatments that are helpful are acupuncture and Chinese herbs; colonics to keep the body cleansed and aid proper digestion; and massage and bodywork. Working with homeopathic remedies is extremely helpful at this time. In my own experience, I was given my constitutional remedy when I first started missing menstrual periods, and this alleviated all the discomfort and tension. There are several homeopathic remedies that are especially good during the menopause.

Herbs as teas are very important in balancing the hormones. Chaste berry (Vitex) helps to balance both the estrogen and progesterone level and may be mixed with other herbs in combination. The Chinese herb dong quai is also excellent; it may be combined with Chinese licorice as a tea or taken in capsule form, which is not as strong but still works.

A good formula is the following:

Chaste berry (Vitex)	2 parts
Sarsaparilla root	2 parts
Squawvine	2 parts
Black cohosh	1 part
Motherwort	2 parts

Motherwort is especially helpful if there is tension or high blood pressure. Raspberry leaf is another simple tea that balances female hormones.

Nutritional supplements should be taken daily. A blend of calcium, magnesium, and potassium with some vitamin D is essential. Some women do better with just the magnesium and potassium. Calcium is difficult to assimilate in the body, but other minerals help the calcium to assimilate. Be careful of calcium supplements; only use those that are combined with magnesium. Silica is important for the bones as well and may be gotten from shavegrass tea or a silicon-boron supplement. B vitamins are also essential; often they are mixed with other supplements; be cautious of those that have too much vitamin C. Vitamin C is very acid to the body (except in its form as Ester-C) and bioflavonoids (vitamin P) should be used instead. Bioflavonoids are excellent for circulation as well as helping assimilation of vitamin C. The minerals zinc and manganese are often necessary. Zinc is important for the immune system and manganese for the nervous system. Another supplement that is very helpful is some form of GLA (Gamma Linolenic Acid) which contains the essential fatty acids and balances the hormone levels. This is found in evening primrose oil, black currant oil, and borage oil. Free form amino acid capsules are also recommended, especially for those with low blood sugar and those who have had problems with PMS. Vitamin E is not necessary if one is using some form of GLA; the two may be alternated (every other month or every other day).

Diet should be high in leafy green vegetables as kale, collard greens, mustard greens, Swiss chard, turnip greens. These vegetables are high in calcium, magnesium, and potassium. Carrot juice is another good source of calcium; it may be made with celery and parsley and a small amount of turnip, which is very cleansing to the system. Be careful of eating dairy products; they tend to be congesting to the system and have a high fat content. Acidophilus products as yogurt and kefir are better in that the lactose is changed to lactic acid. These may be had on occasion, unless you are allergic to them. Goats milk yogurt is a good substitute and there are good cheeses made from soy. Easy to digest protein sources are recommended for digestion as fresh fish, some fertile eggs, and tofu. If meat is used it should be organic; turkey is high in certain amino acids. Fruits should be used sparingly as they can be too acidic to the body; perhaps a portion once a day or on alternate days if the body is acid. Whole grains are very important in providing essential nutrients and grounding. Eaten in the morning, they help to keep the blood sugar up. Herb teas and coffee substitutes as Roma, Sipp, and Pero should be used along with vegetable juices. In terms of sweets, there are cookies and candy bars in the health food stores made without sugar and with healthy ingredients when one wants a treat.

Regular exercise is most important. Daily stretching and yoga are good but some aerobic type exercise as swimming, dancing, jogging, walking is essential to keep muscles toned up and for circulation. Exercise is relaxing to the nervous system and can be a way of sharing with others. Hiking, swimming, and dancing with others is a nice way to combine exercise with socializing and often provides one with the incentive as well.

Rite of Passage Ceremony

A special ritual to honor the completion of menopause and passage into the wise woman/grandmother phase is very important. The ritual itself and the time women spend preparing for it allows them to get in touch with what it is that they want in this new phase of their lives. It also allows them to formally complete the mother phase by giving thanks for the gifts of this phase.

Bringing women together for this ritual brings up issues important to older women and allows for fears and old beliefs about aging to be dissipated; it allows the new energy to enter.

The rite of passage is conducted after a woman's bleeding is over, usually after she has no bleeding for a year. This indicates that, in fact, she is through the "changes" and has actually entered the new cycle. Some women, however, like to celebrate this rite of passage when they turn fifty, and others at the time of their second Saturn return—the astrological cycle which comes around fifty-six or fifty-seven years of age. This cycle marks the second return of the planet Saturn to its natal position; it signifies that one has been "around the wheel" twice.

In most Native American tribes, the menopause was honored after a woman had stopped her bleeding for a certain number of moon cycles, usually from ten to thirteen cycles. At a special time, she was taken outdoors and she was buried in the earth with the dirt. Sometimes a blanket was thrown over her as well. She was left there overnight and in the morning the older women came to get her. They washed her off, dressed her in ceremonial clothes, prayed to the directions, and she was then given a new name by the woman who was the head of her clan. She shared with the women what her dreams had been the previous night and she was often initiated into a particular medicine society at this time as well. When the ceremonies were completed, there was dancing, drumming, celebration, and feasting with corn cakes and other special foods.

In my own work with women, we do a ceremony once a year to initiate new women into the Crone/Grandmother phase. It takes place in November or late October, during the time of Scorpio, the time of the crone and the Dark Goddess. We call it a "Crone Rite of Passage" or "Initiation into the Grandmother Circle." There are always some new women there to be initiated into the crone phase as well as women who have been initiated in years past. There are often younger women too, who are interested in the discussions and who have come to honor the new grandmothers. In the morning we discuss the role of the older woman in society, the freedom, the wisdom, the creativity, and the wildness of the Crone/Grandmother; we also discuss ways of balancing the body physiologically with herbs and nutritional supplements. We drum, chant, and allow our energies to flow.

In the afternoon I conduct the rite of passage ceremony, often with the help of other women who have gone through the ceremony before. All the women are told to bring some special ceremonial dress or robe for the occasion and also any special objects to place on the altar. The altar for this ceremony has objects in the four directions. The feathers in the east may be from birds sacred to the crone as owl feathers and wings (owls have vision at night when it is dark), and sometimes crow or raven feathers (crows and ravens are associated with night magic and wisdom). The candles in the south may be black, for this dark moon phase. The water in the west may be in a special black bowl; the crystal in the north may be smoky quartz or perhaps obsidian. There would also be pictures of grandmothers and statues of crone goddesses. In the east there is a bowl of blue corn seeds which are used later in the ceremony.

Everyone is smudged and then I call in the directions, often calling in a crone goddess for each direction. For example, in the east I might call in Kali, the Hindu goddess, to honor the Orient and the Eastern peoples; in the south, Oya, the African goddess, to honor the peoples of the south; in the west, Spider Grandmother, the Native American goddess, to honor the peoples of the Western world; and in the north, Hella from Scandinavia, to honor the Northern peoples. Sometimes I call in Hecate at the end, since she is the most well known of the crone goddesses.

Oh, Kali, I call you from the eastern gate, Goddess of creation and destruction, you who dance in the graveyards, you who know of the transformation we are going through today. Be with us and help us, Kali Ma.

Oya, dark African mother, you who stand at the frontier between life and death, insatiable in your quest for truth, we call you at the southern gate.

Spider Grandmother, creatress of the fire that lights the dark western gate, we ask that you be present here with us today.

Hella, Scandinavian mistress of the dead, you who ride through the Black Forest, we invoke your ancient wisdom.

Hecate, Crone Goddess of the dark moon, you who stand at the crossroads of humanity, come into our circle and bless us.

After the goddesses are invoked, one woman starts chanting "Ancient Mother" very softly and all join her. While the chanting is going on, the High Priestess or Crone/Grandmother leading the ritual gives each woman who is being initiated three blue corn seeds. When the chanting is over, she instructs the women on the meaning of the seeds:

The first seed is for all the ovum that have passed through you.
The second seed is for any physical children you have birthed.
The third seed is for all your creative projects.

Then the women go round the circle, each one invoking some attribute of the Crone/Grandmother or some crone goddess that is special to her. (Prior to this ceremony, we have spent the morning discussing the attributes of the Crone/Grandmother and her responsibilities.) Those already initiated may share stories of their own initiation or wisdom they want to give to the new crones.

Then each woman being initiated rises from her place in the circle; she goes to the end of the circle where there is a bowl. Into this bowl she places the seeds after she has given thanks and made prayers for all three seeds. Meanwhile, the rest of the women present form a bridge with their hands. She goes under this bridge after making her prayers. When she comes out, one woman gives her a sip from a goblet of grape juice or wine, symbolizing the blood, and another woman gives her a taste of bee pollen or honey, for the sweetness of this phase. Then she pronounces her new name and all chant the name back to her.

After all the new Crone/Grandmothers have been honored, we go outside and plant the seeds; we celebrate the new Grandmothers with chanting, dancing, and drumming. Special ceremonial foods as corn bread, fresh seasonal vegetables garnished with flowers, and herb teas as sarsaparilla root and raspberry leaf may be shared.

Chants for Crone Ceremony

Ancient Mother
Ancient Mother, I hear you calling,
Ancient Mother, I hear your song,
Ancient Mother, I hear your laughter,
Ancient Mother, I taste your tears.

Ancient Mother, I hear you calling,
Ancient Mother, I hear your song,
Ancient Mother, I hear your laughter,
Ancient Mother, I touch your ground.

(Tape: *The Giveaway*,
Ojai Foundation)

We Are the Old Women
We are the Old women,
We are the New women,
We are the same women,
Wiser than before.

We Are Sisters on a Journey
We are sisters on a journey,
Singing in the Sun,
Singing in the darkest night,
The healing has begun, begun,
The healing has begun.

We are sisters on a journey,
Singing now as one,
Remembering the ancient ones,
The Women and their wisdom,
The Women and their wisdom.

The Fire of Freedom (*Starhawk*)
Oh, we will burn with the fire of Freedom,
Truth is the fire that will burn our chains,
We will stop the fires of destruction,
Healing is the fire burning through our veins.

(Tape: *Chants-Ritual Music*,
Reclaiming Collective)

ENDNOTES

1. Walker, Barbara, *The Women's Encyclopedia of Myths and Secrets*, p. 187.

2. *Ibid.*, p. 1077.

3. *Ibid.*

4. *Ibid.*

5. Niethammer, Carolyn, *Daughters of the Earth*, p. 140.

6. *Ibid.*, p. 143.

7. *Ibid.*, p. 144.

8. *Ibid.*

9. *Ibid.*

10. *Ibid.*, p. 145.

11. *Ibid.*

12. Letter from Twylah Nitsch, 12/17/1990.

13. Walker, Barbara, *The Crone*, p. 31.

14. Bachofen, J.J., *Myth, Religion, and Mother Right*, p. 215.

15. See Hood, Sinclair, *The Home of the Heroes: The Aegeans Before the Greeks*; and Hawkes, Jacquetta, *Dawn of the Gods*.

16. Walker, Barbara, *The Crone*, p. 50.

17. *Ibid.*

18. Budge, E., *Dwellers on the Nile*, p. 20.

19. Walker, *The Crone*, p. 51.

20. Scot, Reginald, *Discoveries of Witchcraft*, p. 550.

21. Walker, *The Crone*, p. 76.

22. Sams, Jamie, *Sacred Path Cards*, p. 239.

23. *Menopause: a self-care manual*, Santa Fe Health Education Project, p. 10.

Death

If birth is life's greatest mystery, death certainly is the enigma most difficult to encompass. A birth is a joyous occasion, but how many people think of death as a "celebration?" If at a birth we wonder where the "I" originates, at death the equally unanswerable question arises, where does the "I" go? Each culture and each religion grapples with this conundrum. The gift of life seems so pleasurable that we accept and welcome a new birth. But what happens when that precious gift is taken away? Why do we die? Where do we go when we die? Is there a life after death? Is there a soul, and if so, is that soul reincarnated in an earthly body?

Americans as a society don't have satisfactory answers to the query of what happens after death, although in this century we are surrounded by death and the news of deaths. With the advent of television we were able to view the assassination of the Kennedys, see the riots at Watts, and follow the progress of the continuing horrors of the wars in Southeast Asia, Africa, Afganistan, and the Middle East. The battlefield is no longer an unknown place of carnage able to be romanticized or glorified by the average civilian because that "average civilian" sees depicted all too graphically on TV what happens in a war zone. We all view these death scenes and disasters nightly on television, but we see them in our comfortable living rooms projected via a small, depersonalized screen so that actual events become less real than the more vivid violence of so many films. Earlier in 1991, the "civilized" nations of the world's invasion of Iraq was presented as a mini-series complete with catchy titles such as "Desert Storm" or "Destiny in the Desert." Here we watched formidable and highly skilled weapons being launched, but were not allowed to see the human misery they caused their targets.

Individual death is not a reality integrated into the average American's life. Elisabeth Kübler-Ross, writing in 1975, answered her own question, "Why is it so hard to die?" by saying, "It is difficult to accept death in this society because it is so unfamiliar." Real death, that is, the death of family and friends was, until very recently, something white America did not see. Only the scourge of AIDS, the rise in victims of cancer, and the devastation caused by hard drugs have allowed the average person to witness firsthand the death of loved ones. Our elderly no longer remain in the home, but are whisked away to nursing homes at the first sign of incompetence or senility. Often they themselves choose to live in special retirement communities removing themselves from effective and affective connection with their children or grandchildren.

Now, in the last decade of the twentieth century, the family unit, the "nuclear family" as it has come to be called, seems to be rapidly disappearing. Not only do three or four generations not live together in one house or one town, but even two generations rarely remain together. Children are expected to leave home early and elderly parents are expected to stay decently out of sight. Only recently has there been a rise in the number of children remaining at home after high school or college, and this trend seems to be the result of inflation rather than affection. Our society has become so fragmented that people are now segregated by age, race, education, wealth, and even sexual persuasion and gender. The great migrations westward and southward since World War II have split generations of families. The death of one's mother or father often not only occurs in a hospital, but the hospital itself is in another state or another part of the country.

As we have seen with other areas of life—birth and marriage in particular—the trend toward individualism in America reached its apogee in the 1960s and is now gradually reversing itself. The work of Elisabeth Kübler-Ross has done a great deal to explore the question of death in our society, especially by bringing the subject out from its taboo status into the realm of discourse. She feels our death taboo partly comes from the fact that people routinely die in hospitals. The hospital as the site of birth and death is a twentieth century phenomenon. Anyone familiar with the nineteenth century novel will recall the very affecting deathbed scenes that occurred in most novels. Even nineteenth century novelists themselves weren't exempt from this parade of home deaths. Charlotte Bronte and her pastor father had the misfortune to witness the deaths of her sisters Emily and Anne and her brother Bramwell all in one eight-month period. "A dreary season it was to the family in the parsonage: their usual walks obstructed by the spongy state of the moors—the passing and funeral bells so frequently tolling, and filling the heavy air with their mournful sound—and when the bells were still, the chip chip of the mason as he cut the grave stones in a shed close by."[1]

So far we having been speaking largely about white America. African American, Hispanic, and Asian communities are probably less removed from dealing directly with death than the prevailing culture. However, as "minorities" become integrated into the dominant society, the possibility of their keeping their own customs lessens. White America has a lot to learn from the minority cultures within her borders.

In recent times the appalling spread of HIV virus has caused the gay male community, and now society at large, to approach death and the dying in new ways. Since the disease began its fatal course, few persons are fortunate enough not to have mourned the death of at least one loved one from AIDS; for those who live in the gay community, the '80s has been one long funeral. In the San Francisco Bay Area, where I lived until recently, AIDS has caused the gay community to devise new humanistic, spiritual, and ritualistic ways to encompass the death of friends and lovers. Home care for the dying has become common. Organizations such as Hospice and Shanti regularly work with people who wish to die at home; they also teach relatives how to manage their loved ones' disease so as to keep them painfree and spiritually alert. Obituaries in the gay press are written in personal terms by loved ones as opposed to the formal death notices seen in the daily press.

As death again becomes an acceptable stage of life rather than its unmentionable end, more and more people are adopting a hands-on policy with the deaths of their loved ones. Last week I talked to a woman whose father had recently died. The father wanted to die at home, so at the time of his death his wife and two adult daughters were in attendance. The family wasn't religious and had no predetermined ritualistic way to deal with the body. Nonetheless, they decided that they wished to prepare and dress the body themselves prior to cremation. One daughter was appalled by seeing her father's mouth hanging open in an expression of horror. She decided to put the silk scarf she was wearing (one with a bright leopardskin pattern) under his jaw and tie it over his head. Then she felt the bow on the top of his head looked inappropriate so she removed the scarf. Some hours later, the daughter looked at her father again and noticed that his expression had changed; now his open mouth had relaxed into a slight smile. This physiological response seemed miraculous to her and she felt that her father accepted his death and was blessed. The entire experience of laying out the body was healing for the mother and daughters in a way that having a funeral home perform these functions would not have been.

Preparations for Crossing Over

For women, especially, preparation for crossing over is important because women throughout history have been acknowledged as having a special understanding of the mystery of death. They instinctively know that those who are terminally ill and have a limited amount of time left on this plane should be allowed to do all those things they enjoy the most or that they never did previously. Walks in the woods, painting, and music, thinking about and remembering their past, communicating with dear ones—so many pleasures we deny ourselves each day in order to work at our jobs or take care of practical matters—now become all important. How vital it is to acknowledge people we care about but to whom we have never expressed our love. The end of life is a time to speak openly to those with whom we have unfinished business. Each day can now be lived to its fullest, as though it were our last.

Thinking about how we would like to live the last weeks or days of our lives raises questions of priorities. Perhaps we should always live as though each day were our last so that we could fulfill our profoundest desires and communicate our deepest emotions. As the native people of this continent often say each morning when they pray, "This would be a good day to die."

At each moment in our lives then, especially in the second half, we need to be prepared for the transition of entering another plane and another state of consciousness. In the Trukese society in Micronesia, life ends when you are forty and then death begins.[2] In America, we try to hide aging—spending vast amounts of money and energy on plastic surgery, make-up for wrinkles, hair coloring, and estrogen therapy for menopause. Better to respect and learn from the elders of tribal peoples. Before we can begin preparations for our transition, we should acknowledge the wisdom handed down by the elders so that we will not fear this latter stage of life so much.

Perhaps the most important thing we can do each day is to be open and clear in all our relationships. If there is someone for whom we have angry thoughts, with whom we are unhappy, we need to share this knowledge. If there is someone who has done something to make us feel good, or given us a lot of love and joy, we also need to acknowledge that. If we walk in balance each day with what is in our hearts, sharing openly as though there were no time left, we will never regret or feel guilty about the things we didn't do or say to others.

Another thing we can do each day is to be kind to ourselves and give ourselves daily pleasures—a walk in the woods, listening to some music we love, visiting with friends, or cooking food we enjoy. Too many people in our society are caught in the "fast lane." Working, going to meetings, classes, fulfilling family obligations keep us constantly out in the world with very little time for reflection and introspection. This fast pace often leads to illness so that one has to slow down and look within. It is easier to go willingly, as Inanna did when she journeyed to the underworld, than to be forced by illness or catastrophe to take stock of oneself.

If we are helping a friend prepare for crossing over, we want to make her/him physically comfortable in every way. This usually involves remaining in her/his own home if that is possible or in another loving supportive environment. Having ceremonial objects close at hand such as special crystals and feathers as well as favorite photographs or paintings is another important consideration. I remember years ago visiting a friend who was dying from Hodgkin's disease. Her husband had set up a special altar near her bed with many crystals and other medicine objects that friends had brought. This provided her with great solace and was a real focus when she was feeling very ill. She also asked to have some of her favorite foods brought to her—a favorite Chinese dish and a piece of carrot cake. It was as though she were saying good-bye to all her old friends in the food world and thanking them one last time for bringing her pleasure and nourishment. She requested that all her friends have a big party after she had passed on, to celebrate her release from pain and discomfort after so many years. She didn't want any mourning, only rejoicing at this significant rite of passage.

The amount of actual preparation we can do for ourselves depends upon our degree of consciousness and how significant we feel our death to be. There are many spiritual practices to prepare us for our own crossing over. Years ago I was given the *Emerald Tablets of Thoth*. It consists of twelve sections or tablets, one of which is devoted to death and includes a special daily practice that enables one to leave the earthly plane with one's inner or third eye open. Practices of this kind exist in many spiritual traditions.

In certain native societies, many individuals not only know when their own death is coming, but they are able to plan it with the participation of others as well. Murray Trelease reports on his experiences with dying among Alaskan Indians. He says, "In nearly every case, the dying people exhibited a willfulness about their death, their participation in its planning, and the time of its occurrence that showed a remarkable power of personal choice."[3] To know that we have this choice is empowering; and to know that death is just another stage of life, another stage of growth, is comforting.

Rituals and Ceremonies

Funerals and mourning rituals differ in various cultures and religious practices. The intent, however, is always the same: to honor the dead and to give support during the passage to the next stage. Mourning rituals provide help for those who are grieving and an outlet for them to express this grief. Many Native American tribes, as well as other native cultures in Polynesia and Africa, practice wailing and melancholy chants in their ceremonies. It is the Jewish custom to rend clothing before the funeral; this gives the family an opportunity to express their anguish in a ritual way. In other cultures, women cut off their hair as a sign of mourning. In the West, black is the color of mourning and many wear black throughout the year. In the Orient, white is worn.

The *Tibetan Book of the Dead*, the *Bardo Thodol*, is perhaps one of the most complex manuals on death. It describes the various bardos, or intermediary states that one passes through on the way to the next world. There are sections that are read to the dead every night during a forty-nine-day period (after which Buddhists believe rebirth takes place) to help them in their process of cleansing themselves and preparing for the next plane.

At some funerals family members take part in preparing the body and also in digging the grave and placing the coffin in the grave. This provides an avenue for them to express their grief and also gives them time alone to spend with the dead as they lay the person out before the funeral. As painful as this is, it is also a time to share any things that were not shared previously. Also, for some families such as the one I described earlier, laying out the body is a form of healing. People who choose cremation for their loved ones have a ceremony after the cremation with the ashes. These ashes are placed in a ceremonial vessel and often taken to a favorite place in nature where the ashes can be scattered.

Regardless of whether the body is placed in a coffin and lowered into the earth or cremated, the words spoken, songs sung, and the energy of the group is important. This is the time to create a ritual in the spirit of the one who has left, something that is in keeping with the vibratory level of that being. Poems read and prayers given should address the spirit of the departed one.

If this is a traditional funeral performed by a minister, priest, or rabbi, relatives and friends can speak with him beforehand to ask for time to include special songs or prayers. The more active the participation in the funeral by those attending, the more meaningful it will be for all those who are grieving as well as for the one whose spirit is being honored.

I have been to some very poignant death rites. One was for the twenty-one-year-old son of a close friend, whose ashes were brought to the Buddhist center where the rite was held. His parents, brother, and girlfriend spoke to him, addressing him as though he were present. They told him what they would miss about him. Each of them got a chance to share their grief and their feelings with their friends and relatives. His father read a poem he had written for him. Then others in the group offered special poems and prayers. The ceremony was very moving and everyone cried. The true spirit of this being was expressed through those who came to mourn him.

Even if there is a very traditional funeral in which friends do not have the opportunity to share their feelings, it is always possible to conduct an additional ritual for the departed, offering friends a chance to share their own feelings and to receive the support of others who are also grieving. It is important that we plan and conduct rites of passage ceremonies for our dead which emphasize the graduation onto another plane, the last stage of our earth walk.

Outline for Crossing Over Ritual

1. *Choosing or preparing a special place for the ritual.* The site of the ritual should be in keeping with the spiritual beliefs and practices of the departed. If she/he holds religious beliefs, then a place where this religion is practiced is appropriate. If the deceased practiced an earth-based religion, she/he would probably want a ceremony outdoors, weather permitting, near some spot that was special for this soul. The area should be purified and cleansed beforehand. The ritual might also be done in a congenial home, where an appropriate altar could be set up with some of the departed's special objects.

2. *Choosing the person to conduct the ritual.* A High Priestess, Medicine Woman/Man, minister, priest, rabbi, swami, lama, or other person who reflects the departed's beliefs and preferably knew her/him or, at least, some family members personally, would be the most appropriate person to conduct the ceremony.

3. *Laying out the body or preparing the ashes.* Relatives or close friends of the departed often like to lay out the body with special clothes and possessions that she/he may want to take to the next world. There are many reports from close relatives who felt that preparing the body gave them an outlet for their grief and allowed them a last communication with a person they loved. Even if the body of the departed is later cremated, it is important to dress and lay it out properly. After cremation, placing the ashes in a special urn or jar with ceremonial objects nearby would be appropriate.

4. *Conducting the ceremony.* An invocation to bring in the spiritual power—the Goddess/God, Great Mystery, Grandmothers/Grandfathers of the four directions, or any other spiritual guides—is helpful. The person conducting the ceremony should be prepared to give readings and/or poems. Some suggested examples are:

There is a reason for being here
and a reason for leaving:
The world beyond is a land
Of joy and happiness, with youth anew.

As the evergreen grows and prospers,
Both in summer and in winter, year upon year,
So does the soul continue
From life to life.

Growing stronger, wiser and richer.
We call to thee, Dark Mother,
We, your children know that there is naught
To fear in thine embrace,
That a step into thy Darkness,
Is but a step into the Light.

Therefore, in love and without fear,
We commend to thee our sister (or brother).
Take her (him), guard her, guide her,
Admit her to the peace of Summerland,
Which stands between life and life;
And know that our love goes with her.[4]

The moon and the year
travel and pass away:
Also the day, also the wind.
also the flesh passes away
to the place of its quietness.

     Maya[5]

Ah, flowers that we wear,
Ah, songs that we raise,
We are on our way to the realm of the Mystery!
If only for one day,
Let us be together, my friends!
We must leave our flowers behind us,
We must leave our songs:
And yet the earth remains unchanged.
My friends, enjoy! Friends enjoy!

     Aztec[6]

Statements about the departed from close friends and relatives are both important and beautiful. Remembering aloud one's interaction with the deceased and sharing feelings about what she/he has contributed to one's life gives everyone present a chance to unite in love with the departed.

Bringing gifts to the deceased such as evergreen sprigs (symbolizing rebirth), feathers, flowers, seeds for the new cycle, or any appropriate token is an ancient custom and one which shows honor to the departed.

The sharing of songs, dances, and food completes the celebration of this rite of passage and brings together the community of the friends and loved ones of the person who has passed on.

Sample of Ritual for a Funeral or Mourning Ceremony

Participants stand in a circle, after the area has been smudged and cleansed. In the center is an altar with a candle, generally white; flowers; some evergreens (which represent rebirth or continuous life); a clay or ceramic vessel with a silver cord attached; cedar, sage, or incense with an abalone shell and feather for smudging; owl feathers; a snake skin; some seeds; a photograph of the departed one with any of her/his ceremonial objects; and pictures of the goddesses/gods who deal with funerary rites such as Hecate, Inanna, Kali, Pele, Medusa, Isis, Oya, Spider Grandmother, Osiris, Shiva, Odin, or Hades. Often, if the departed has not been connected to any specific spiritual practice or lifestyle, the collection of objects at the altar can be highly eclectic, as long as they truly represent the spirit of the departed person.

The High Priestess, Medicine Woman/Man starts a mourning chant or wailing and all join in. Some movement should be done during the wailing so that the whole body indicates mourning. When the opening chant is completed, the four directions are invoked with goddesses/gods for the four directions or the grandmothers/grandfathers and other meaningful ancient ones.

Now the leader speaks to the group about the purpose of the ritual, about the one who has departed, about death, and how passing on is the final earthly rite of passage.

Next, each person in the circle shares her thoughts about the departed with a poem, song, or personal memories and contributes a feather or flower brought to honor the departed. They may also share their thoughts and experiences with death or their own fears of ultimate dissolution.

Then the closest friend or relative takes the ceramic vessel with the silver cord attached and breaks the cord with a chisel or other instrument (pagans may use an athame). She/he then breaks the vessel and buries the cord and the vessel in the ground, with some prayers about returning to the elements and Mother Earth. Afterwards each person plants a seed in the ground for the new cycle for the departed one, praying as they do so. The High Priestess/Priest covers the seeds with dirt after each person has finished.

At the end, songs are shared and people get up and dance to release energy and celebrate the passing of the beloved one. Often food is shared, then the directions and goddesses are thanked and the circle closed.

Songs

We All Come from the Goddess

We all come from the Goddess,
And to her we shall return,
Like a drop of rain,
Flowing to the ocean.

We all come from the Sun God,
And to him we shall return,
Like a spark of flame,
Floating to the heavens.[7]

(Tape: *From the Goddess—*
On Wings of Song,
Robert Gass)

Wearing My Long Wing (Tail) Feathers

Wearing my long wing (tail) feathers
As I fly,
Wearing my long wing feathers
As I fly,
I circle around, I circle around,
The boundaries of the earth.
I circle around, I circle around,
The boundaries of the earth.[8]

Cross-Cultural Approaches to Crossing Over

In traditional Native American societies, death was seen as a continuity of life, a change of worlds, and not an ending. Many tribes believed there was a place to which one's soul journeyed when one was finished on this plane. Preparations for this transition were begun early, and in many tribes one had the right to determine when and where her/his death might occur.[9]

Sometimes women and men were even conscious participants in their own funerals. When it became apparent that an ill or elderly person was near death, she/he was dressed, painted, and sometimes even partially wrapped up for burial.[10] They were given words of encouragement as they were prepared for death. They were told they were going to rejoin their ancestors, or going to the land of the buffalos. In the Omaha tradition, after a woman had died, she was quickly burned in a shallow grave on a hilltop, and a fire was kept burning on her grave for four nights so its light might cheer her as she traveled to the other world.[11]

In some of the Plains tribes, a woman's favorite horse might be killed so that its tail would be placed near her grave. A prayer would accompany the slaughter of the horse, telling the horse that its owner loved the horse and wanted to take its spirit with her.[12] In the Plains tribes it was customary to give away or destroy all of the dead one's belongings.[13]

The Papagos of southern Arizona burned their homes if someone died there. Often, the dying person was moved from home before death so that the house would not have to be destroyed. When a person was near death, all the relatives gathered round and began a ritual wailing that lasted until the body was buried. The corpse was placed in a pit six or seven inches deep. The dead woman was arranged just as she had been in life, sitting with her knees to the side and surrounded by her pots and baskets. The grave was not filled with dirt but roofed over like a house. After the burial, one of the elders made a short speech in which the deceased was asked not to return to the earth and frighten her relatives. The Papago believed that the souls of the dead could fly back to earth in the form of owls whenever they felt a longing for one of their relatives.[14]

Anything to do with death was feared by the Navajos; when someone was very close to death, all but the immediate family left the area. If the person died inside the hogan, they burned the hogan and moved to another spot. If it was possible, they had an outsider bury the body; if not, four of the mourners bathed the corpse, dressed it in good clothing, including whatever jewelry the person had worn. The body was hidden in a crevice and piled over with stones, dirt, and sticks. When the burial attendants rejoined the rest of the family, they all mourned for four days, eating little and doing little work. For a long time, the name of the dead one was not mentioned, as they did not want to irritate the soul or compel it to linger about the family.[15]

The Hopis also believed that the souls of the dead lived on; they felt these spirits were benevolent and brought rain to those still living. When a Hopi woman died, her hair was washed with yucca suds; a thin white cloth symbolizing clouds was put over her face, and she was sewn, in a sitting position, in her white cotton marriage blanket, which was tied with a knotted belt. Later, it was thought that the spirit of the woman would move along through the sky as a cloud, the small raindrops falling through the loosely woven blanket, and the big raindrops falling from the fringes of the belt.[16]

In addition to believing that the souls of the dead lived on, Native Americans ritually mourned each person who died. Women were the chief mourners in the tribes and practiced loud moaning and wailing. Wailing was not considered as painful as silent sorrow.[17]

In addition to individual mourning, many tribes also held a yearly ritual to mourn their dead. The Cree in central Canada intoned melancholy songs and danced. Each person got up and danced, one after another, until morning, by which time they had all given vent to their grief and sadness. This provided a yearly catharsis for the tribe and allowed them to return to their lives refreshed.[18] The Yumas and Cahuillas, in southwestern United States, also held annual tribal mourning ceremonies. The Cahuilla invited neighbors from other villages and held a big feast in the ceremonial house. Families of people who had died during the year made images of the dead out of cloth stuffed with grass and topped by human hair wigs. On the last day of the week-long ceremony, female relatives of those who had crossed over brought the effigies out and led the procession. Later the effigies were burned.[19]

Through these annual mourning ceremonies tribal people released their grief and were provided an outlet in song, dance, and ceremony to express grief and sadness. In many other cultures, there are also special rituals done for the dying and group mourning. In Hawaii, among the native inhabitants, friends and relatives are called to have a wailing procession, followed by a big luau to honor all those who carried the casket, made the coffin, and dug the burial hole. Children are always included and thus learn early that death is a part of life.[20] The Chinese do a lot of wailing and weeping at the funeral. They burn paper money in order to give the dead person some money to spend in the other world. They also believe that unfriendly spirits are present at the funeral and thus they ask the living to turn their backs to the casket so that the evil spirits will not follow them home.[21]

The Japanese practice certain rituals connected with death as well. The Buddhist tradition has them observe religious practices in order to assure the spirit's travel to the other world. If the family neglects to do this, the spirits return and "nudge" them. One of their rituals is the bathing of the body of the one who has crossed over. Years ago, the body was kept outside because of the stench and the family stayed up all night with it, giving rise to the idea of the "wake." After the funeral there was a big feast given for all the friends and helpers, and when this was over, the family was allowed to eat meat again.[22]

ENDNOTES

1. Gaskell, Mrs., *Charlotte Bronte*, Penguin Books, p. 172.

2. Kübler-Ross, Elisabeth, *Death as the Final Stage of Growth*, p. 29.

3. Trelease, Murray, "Dying Among Alaskan Indians: A Matter of Choice," in Kübler-Ross, *Death as the Final Stage of Growth*, pp. 33–37.

4. Farrar, Stewart, *Eight Sabbats for Witches*, Washington, Phoenix Publishing, 1981.

5. Bierhorst, John, ed., *In the Trail of the Wind: American Indian Poems and Ritual Orations*, p. 91.

6. *Ibid.*, p. 101.

7. Kealoha, Anna, *Songs of the Earth*, Celestial Arts, Berkeley, CA, 1989, p. 169.

8. *Ibid.*, p. 164.

9. Beck & Walters, *The Sacred*, p. 205.

10. Niethammer, Carolyn, *Daughters of the Earth*, p. 255.

11. *Ibid.*

12. *Ibid.*

13. *Ibid.*, p. 256.

14. *Ibid.*, p. 257.

15. *Ibid.*

16. *Ibid.*, p. 258.

17. *Ibid.*, p. 252.

18. *Ibid.*, p. 254.

19. *Ibid.*

20. Kübler-Ross, p. 29.

21. *Ibid.*, p. 30.

22. *Ibid.*

Yearly Rituals:
Equinox, Solstice and
Cross-Quarter Days

While the moon and her cycles divide up the month and provide the basis for monthly rituals, the sun and its relation to the earth, set the stage for the rituals we do during the year. Because of the earth's rotation on her axis, the sun and other celestial bodies appear to move through the sky from east to west along certain paths. The sun slips backward (eastward) every day against the daily (westward) motion of the stars.

As the sun shifts among the background of stars, (approximately one degree per day), it shifts its position along the horizon as it rises and sets.[1] If one observes the sun every day from the same place, within a year's time, there would be a sixty degree total angular swing between extreme positions along the horizon. The sun travels south in the fall and winter until it appears to stop for several days around December 21. (*Solstice* means "sun stopping" in Latin.) At this time its angular position is thirty degrees south of the horizon; this angle is termed the azimuth.[2] Many native peoples feared that if the sun did not begin to move again, the fields would freeze and all living things would die. They therefore designed elaborate ceremonies to entreat the sun to move northward again. Similarly, in summer, when the sun reaches its northernmost point and the earth is hot and dry, there are ceremonies to entreat the sun to move south again. In terms of ritual, these two points, Winter and Summer Solstice are the strongest times of the year. The Hopis say that the sun is inclined to wander and must be encouraged to stay on his course.[3]

On its journey from south to north and north to south, the sun reaches an angle where the days and nights on earth are equal; these are referred to as Fall Equinox and Spring Equinox. The equinox points are turning points in the seasonal cycle; in the Northern Hemisphere, Fall Equinox is a time when the weather is getting colder, plants are dying, and a taste of the cold winter months is present. In spring, on the other hand, the warmth of summer and the first buds of flowers are experienced. Both of these points represent changes in nature and thus, within each of us. We move to an inner place in fall to prepare for the winter months, and to an outer place in spring to celebrate the renewal of life and warmth.

Many Native American societies had a Sun Priest who made calculations each day on the sun's position and marked these on rocks to determine times for planting and ceremonies. These were the most ancient calendars. Later, sacred sites were built where the angle of the sun could be seen each day and where the sun hit certain places on the solstice and equinox. The Anasazi culture of the southwestern United States, precursor to the Pueblo civilization, has several of these sites. One that has been studied much is Fajada Butte in Chaco Canyon, New Mexico. On Fajada Butte, the position of the noonday sun is observed. There is a spiral hidden between three large stone slabs. About noon on Summer Solstice, sunlight passes between two of the three upright slabs that lean back against the ledge upon which the spiral is carved. The spot of light lengthens into a dagger shape and begins to move slowly downward through the center of the spiral. Eighteen minutes later, the streak has moved through the spiral and faded away. A few days before and after the solstice, the sun dagger falls to the east of the spiral.[4]

In the Hopi tribe in Arizona, shrines are erected at spots on the horizon where the sun rises or sets at specific times. Prayer sticks are planted in each shrine the day the sun rises or sets over it. Through these observations, the Hopis determine the dates for their most important ceremonies—the Wuwuchim (beginning of the ceremonial year when the Kachinas return), Soyal (winter solstice ceremony), and Niman (time when the Kachinas return).[5]

At Hovenweep National Monument, another Anasazi sacred place, there are small ports or loopholes in the buildings which provide for light and ventilation. During the day, bright spots of light move along the opposite wall. The port through which the light passes and the place the spots of light fall, depend directly on the time of year and the time of day.[6] In this way, solstices and equinoxes were timed.

Other Native American structures that worked like a calendar in measuring the sun's angle are the medicine wheels, which were primarily built by the Plains tribes. Medicine wheels were often laid out in a pattern that converged toward a central cairn (pile of rocks) similar to the spokes of a wheel. They may have several other cairns along with them and sometimes circles of rock as well. The central cairns were often three or four yards high and ten yards across, requiring tons of rock to be carried to the site.[7] One of the best examples of these medicine wheels is the Bighorn Medicine Wheel in Wyoming, which is built at an altitude of 10,000 feet, above the timberline and excellent for observing the sky. An astronomer, John Eddy, investigated the Bighorn wheel on Summer

Solstice and found that the first rays of the rising sun appeared just above the center of the wheel. He also observed sunset on the same day and went on to study other medicine wheels on the Great Plains.[8]

In early European culture, the Celts believed the alternation of day and night, light and darkness, posited the fundamental duality of being—north/south, dark/light, death/life. The dead of night was felt to be closer to the other world—a person born during the night can see ghosts and phantoms undetected by children born during the daylight hours. In Wales, January was called the "black month" while in Scotland, Cornwall, and Brittany, November was given that honor.

It is believed the Celts followed a tree calendar, with the names of months corresponding to the names of trees and also to the consonants of the alphabet. Their year began at the Winter Solstice and then had thirteen months of twenty-eight days each. The Coligny Calendar (first century B.C.) shows a lunar month with the regular lunation of 29-1/2 days. However, since the letters on the calendar are in Roman script engraved on a brass tablet, the calendar is thought to represent the romanizing of the native Druidic religion. The twenty-eight-day cycle can be considered the true lunar month, not only in the astronomical sense of the moon's revolutions in relation to the sun, but also in the mystic sense that the moon, as woman, has a woman's menstrual period of twenty-eight days.[9]

Native Solstice Celebrations

For Native Americans the most important seasonal ritual appears to be Winter Solstice. Some tribes as the Chumash in California saw this as a particularly dangerous time where all supernatural powers were mustered to encourage the sun to move northward and restore balance to the world.[10] On the actual Winter Solstice, the Chumash remained indoors so that they would not be eaten by the sun at the end of his journey. After the sun's turn north, they celebrated with public and private rituals.[11] During the first day of the Winter Solstice ceremony, the people settled all their debts, in order to approach the New Year with a clean slate. On the second day, a ceremony was conducted to pull the sun northward again. A hole about twelve to eighteen inches across had been dug in the plaza. On the afternoon of the solstice, the chief priest, called Image of the Sun, and his twelve assistants called Rays of the

Sun, erected a sunstick in the hole they had prepared. The sunstick was a fifteen- to eighteen-inch long stick with a stone disk on top. In the middle of the afternoon the Image of the Sun appeared with his twelve assistants. The twelve Rays of the Sun held a goose or eagle feather from the sunstick in his hands. At a certain time they tossed the feathers in the air and let them fall in simulation of rain. The sun priest then chanted, "It is raining! You must go into the house!" The Rays of the Sun closed this portion of the ritual by dancing. Later that night the priests and the people danced around decorated poles called sun poles. Until midnight they danced in a clockwise or sunwise fashion; after midnight they danced in anti-sunwise direction. The dancing stopped at sunrise and the people assembled around the sunstick to implore the sun to return and enter the axis of the earth. That evening the Dance of the Widows was performed for any women or girls who had become widows or orphans during the year. Everyone wept in memory of those who had died and for the passing year. The final morning the sunstick was taken down and placed in a box inlaid with shell. These were put away until the next year.[12]

The Hopis and Zunis also make prayer sticks to the sun at the Winter and Summer Solstice. These prayer sticks or *bahos* were made of sticks of cottonwood a few inches long and a little larger than a pencil in diameter. One is male and one female; they have eagle or turkey feathers attached so that the prayers might reach their destination, the sun. After daybreak on the solstice, the priests climb to the shrine, which was open to the east and had no roof. The prayer sticks were planted in the sandy floor of the shrine.[13]

In the Hopi villages, part of the solstice ceremony which takes place in the kiva involves an enactment of the sun's indecision about assuming his proper yearly path. The chief of one of the societies carries a shield, on which is a painting of the sun. On his head he wears a tablet decorated with the rain cloud symbol. Novices who are being initiated into the society stand at the four cardinal points and chant invocations to the gods for rain and good crops. Then the shield bearer mimics the sun, moving first to the north and then to the south where groups of singers greet him. Present at this ritual are a few women who took part in the ceremony, a few male society members, and several young initiates. The following morning at dawn, the ceremony was done publicly. At sunrise a masked god carrying symbols of the sun entered the pueblo. Two men dressed as women walked with him carrying trays in which were ears of corn set on end and arranged in a circle. Fertility elements are a strong part of the ritual. In this way, the Hopi emphasize the connection between the sun's return to the north and the abundance of food.[14]

At Zuni, fertility rituals involve planting prayer sticks in the field at Winter Solstice. Families deposit their prayer plumes in shallow excavations in their own fields. The plumes remain uncovered until sunset the following day so that the Sun Father may receive the prayers breathed into the plumes. There is also a strong emphasis on lighting the new fire so that the new year gets off to a good start. On the day before, the fire maker visits every house and collects a piece of cedar which has been prayed over with prayers that the crops will thrive. Ten days after the Winter Solstice a new fire ceremony is held, during which there is much dancing. Kachinas visit each kiva and present seeds to each person for later planting.[15]

Cross-Quarter Days

In between each solstice and equinox falls a day which has special ritual significance in many of the cultures where the Goddess was worshipped. It is felt that on these days the energy inaugurated at the solstice and equinox becomes manifest. In the Demeter/Persephone myth, Persephone is born at the Winter Solstice; at Candlemas, Feb. 2, she is still an infant; at Spring Equinox she is a growing child, and at Beltane, May 1, she comes of age and into her menarche. At Summer Solstice she discovers and enters the labyrinth; on Lammas, Aug. 1, she reaches Hecate in the underground; at the Fall Equinox Demeter mourns for her daughter and all vegetation dies; at All Hallows, Oct. 31, Demeter finds Persephone. This is the time when the living and the dead are reunited; it has been considered the end of the year in Wiccan traditions. At Winter Solstice, Persephone returns from the underworld and is reborn.

The Demeter/Persephone story was celebrated in Greece in the Eleusinian Mysteries. Persephone seems to embody the vegetation, and particularly the corn, which is buried under the soil for months during the winter and sprouts again in the spring. Demeter represents the earth, which dies, is reborn, and is united with Persephone, the new corn. This myth is similar to the Egyptian one of Isis and Osiris, the Syrian Astarte

and Adonis, and the Phrygian Cybele and Attis. In these myths, the male god represents the vegetation and the corn; he dies each year and then is reborn and united with his female consort, who symbolizes the earth.

Thus, the waxing part of the cycle begins at Winter Solstice where the days lengthen, the warmth returns, seeds are planted and blossom. At Summer Solstice, the waning cycle is inaugurated; the mature crops are harvested, the energy is concentrated back into the roots, the earth is barren and dies, the coldness and darkness of winter sets in.

Ceremonies for the Eight Turning Points in the Year

Winter Solstice

This ceremony was the most important to the Native Americans as it marks the beginning of a cycle. The light returns as the sun shifts and starts to move northward again. We look within ourselves now to find the new source of light and regeneration. The goddess Persephone is reunited with her mother; the Christ child emerges from his mother's womb.

At the time of the Winter Solstice, the sun appears to stand still for four days. Native Americans refer to this time period as Earth Renewal and spend the four days in prayer and fasting, remaining close to nature and refraining from many activities, in order to give the earth a rest and pray for the sun to move on. This is a time of year when all tribal medicine bundles from clans and secret societies are opened and renewed. They are usually placed around the fire the night before the solstice, opened up, and blessed.

In Europe, the tradition of the yule log is celebrated on Winter Solstice. A special log is brought in and placed on the hearth where it glows for the twelve nights of the holiday season. After that, it is kept in the house all year to protect the home and its inhabitants from illness and any adverse conditions. The yule log is the counterpart of the midsummer bonfires, which were held outdoors on Summer Solstice, the longest night. It is also customary to place mistletoe around the fire, which is the plant that grew on the oak tree, sacred to the Druids, the priests of the old Celts. Mistletoe has many uses and is thought to help women to conceive. The Christmas tree also dates from old

European or pagan rituals; it was the time to celebrate the renewal of all earth, and greens were used as the symbol—branches of pine, cedar, and juniper. Red candles are symbolic of the fire returning, the fire and heat of the sun as the days begin to lengthen.

Ritual

The night before the solstice is a good time to celebrate the darkness and the emerging light. This can be done where each person holds a candle which she lights and then offers her prayers for the returning light. Each woman may also lie in a womblike posture and one woman, impersonating the Goddess, may walk around and touch each one. As each woman rises and is born from the womb, she prays for what she wants in the new cycle, including any prayers for the earth.

Another way to celebrate the night prior to the solstice is to conduct a women's moon ceremony or a sweat lodge. The moon ceremony is a balance to the solar force that is being celebrated. Here is a special moon ceremony for solstices and equinoxes that was taught to me and several other women by Oh Shinnah.

Moon Ceremony

Women find a special rock that they bring to the ceremony; this can be a small or medium-sized rock that has been purified in water and sea salt. (Later they then can bring the rocks back to their own land if they choose.) After they are smudged and the directions called in, one woman, who is in charge of the ceremony, holds an eagle feather (or another feather) and points with it to the spot where each rock should be placed. The rocks form a semicircular altar which is the moon altar. This is located between the women and the fire, which has been ritually started by one of the women, who is the firekeeper. In front of the moon altar is a cloth on which the women may place any of their ceremonial objects that they want blessed. These objects usually remain on the cloth overnight and are taken back the next day after the ceremonies are completed.

Next the High Priestess or Medicine Woman leading the ceremony talks about the significance of the light returning and of a special medicine bundle that will be made while they pray to Grandmother Moon. The leader has made the bundle and already placed in it some wood from a tree that has been hit with lightning, along with cornmeal, tobacco, a crystal, and any other objects she feels are important. As the women begin chanting to the moon, she digs a hole in the earth with a crystal (in the south) and places in it some cornmeal and a small crystal or star rock. Three other women then dig holes, with the same crystal, to the west, north, and east, and also place some cornmeal and a small crystal or star rock in them. During the second round of chanting to the moon, the bundle is passed around the circle and each woman places an object in it. It is then returned to the Medicine Woman who ties it up. During the third repetition of chanting, each woman breathes her prayers into the bundle as it is passed around. Then the leader talks about how the bundle will be used for healing.

There are many moon chants that may be used. Here is one from Brooke Medicine Eagle's *A Gift of Song*:

Neesa, Neesa, Neesa,
Neesa, Neesa, Neesa,
Neesa, Neesa, Neesa,
Gay-we-o, Gay-we-o.

(This is repeated four times, then one group may sing Neesa, Neesa, Neesa, while the other chants Gay-we-o, Gay-we-o.)

Morning Ceremony

In the morning at dawn, an Earth Renewal ceremony is done. The following ceremony was taught to me by Oh Shinnah, who learned it as part of her native heritage.

All present stand in a circle around the fire. This ceremony is done for women and men, so if the group is just women, women may be chosen for the two male roles. The oldest woman and youngest maiden of consciousness stand in the west. The oldest man stands in the east and the youngest man of consciousness enters from the north. All are smudged before beginning the ritual.

The oldest woman moves clockwise or sunwise inside the circle and digs a hole with a crystal; she places corn seeds in the hole and prays for the seeds to grow and ripen. Next the maiden enters and sprinkles pollen on the seeds, praying for the unborn and all that is uncompleted. Meanwhile, the youngest boy has started his run for the sun around the circle in a clockwise direction with water in his mouth. He has to time it so that he enters the circle right after the maiden sprinkles in the pollen. He lets the water out of his mouth onto the seeds and pollen offering a prayer for rain. He returns to the circle next to the oldest man in the east. The oldest man then enters and covers the seeds, offering prayers to remember our finite nature.

The person conducting the ceremony then hands each person a pinch of tobacco, which is held in the left hand until it is her time to walk to the fire pit and say her prayers. Praying out loud or silently, she then throws the tobacco into the fire. For people not able to be present at the ceremony, a small red tobacco bundle may be made and thrown into the fire with prayers for them. When all have completed their prayers the following song, which is a greeting song, is chanted.

Hey, Hey, Hey, Hey, Hey, Ungua (4 times)
Ungua, Ungua.[16]

(This song can be heard on the tape *In Vision, Songs of Spirit*.)

More chants are sung after which the leader closes the circle. This is the time to break the fast (for those who have been fasting for four days). Corn bread and light foods are shared.

Here is another song appropriate for the Winter Solstice. (It is written by Charlie Murphy and is found on the tape *Canticles of Light* produced by Art Front Music, P.O. Box 12188, Seattle, WA 98103.)

One planet is turning, circle on her path around the sun.
Earth Mother is calling her children home.
Light is returning, even though this is the darkest hour.
No one can hold back the dawn.
Let's keep it burning, let's keep that flame of hope alive.
Make safe the journey through the storm.[17]

Candlemas—February 2

Candlemas or St. Brigit's Day is one of the four Celtic fire festivals which fall on the cross-quarter days, six weeks between the solstices and equinoxes. Candlemas is a time when the light of rebirth grows stronger; it is a time for retreat and rekindling of the inner fire. Brigit is the triple goddess of the flame.

Her fire was carried from the land of Brigantia on the British Isles to Kildare, not far from Dublin in Ireland. The Daughters of the Flame, nine sacred Virgins who could be looked on by no man, tended her fire; later it was tended by the Christian sisters when she became Saint Brigit (or Bridget or Brigid). Brigit's fires are the fires of purification and healing. At a certain point the flames were extinguished by the church who called it "pagan."

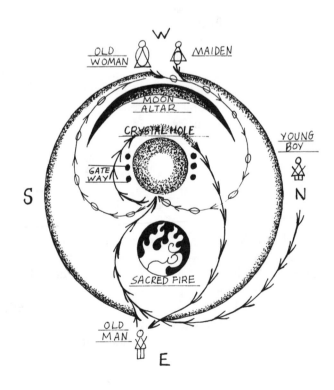

There were also many wells and springs of healing throughout the countryside that were dedicated to Brigit. These waters were waters of renewal as it is said that Brigit cured all, including lepers and the impotent.[18] Brigit was also the goddess called upon by poets and singers as she revealed how sounds could be turned into written marks and thus understood by others miles away.[19]

Candlemas is the time of the feast of poets, of the nine muses. It is a time in Wicca when priestesses are initiated into the coven. It can be a time when women (and men) dedicate themselves to the Goddess.

The emphasis here is on purification from the dark forces of winter. Traditionally, all the candles that were to be used during the year were brought to the church on Candlemas. The Christians say that Candlemas (forty days after Christmas, or Christ's birth) is when Mary presented Christ in the temple. It is important to have candles on the altar, preferably white, for each direction. Also white or gold candles for each woman present.

Ritual

After the sacred fire is built and everyone smudged, the High Priestess or leader calls in the directions. She may call in fire goddesses for the four directions, as for example:

> To the East, I call in Erato, the Greek muse of lyric poetry and inspiration
> To the South, Pele, Hawaiian Goddess of the volcanos,
> To the West, Oya, African Goddess of purification,
> To the North, Brigit of the Holy Well and Sacred Flame.

Next, each woman lights a candle and as she does so, she asks to let go of the darkness of the winter months that she has carried with her. She then invokes a goddess whose energy she wants to work with in the next cycle. She may speak about the goddess, sing a song, do a dance, or read a poem in honor of that goddess. She may also wear any costume or mask representing that goddess.

When all have shared their goddess, the High Priestess talks about Brigit, followed by singing, dancing, and eating special food. This is a time when the movement is toward spring and the creative spirit, so individual creative contributions from each person present are especially welcome.

Chants

The Way to the Well
We will never
never lose our way
to the well
of her memory
and the power
of her Living Flame.
It will rise,
It will rise again.

> (Tape: *The Way to the Well*, Starhawk)

Blessings of the Goddess
May the blessings of the Goddess rest upon you.
May her peace abide in you.
May her presence illuminate your heart.
Now and forever more.[20]

> (Tape: *Songs to the Goddess*, Sonoma County Birth Network)

Spring Equinox

Spring Equinox is a time when the day and night force are equal, when plants begin to burst forth from the earth, when leaves appear on the trees, and the movement of insects is felt again. Spring is the time when Persephone returns from the underworld as a young girl, and mother and daughter play together out in the fields and usher in the new growth. It is a time for each of us to honor the child within and give voice to that child. It is also a time for each of us to cleanse our bodies and spirits in preparation for the rebirth.

The celebration of Easter occurs close to the time of this equinox. *Oestre* or *Eostar* was a feast of the goddess Ishtar/Astarte/Esther and celebrated her rebirth. The egg was used as a symbol for Eostar as it represented the birth of the Goddess and of all nature.

Prior to the equinox it is important that each woman do some individual cleansing, including a spring fast, and colonic or herbal enemas. Letting go of old material in the body precipitates the letting go of old emotions stored up in the dark of winter.

The night before the equinox, or that day, it is good to do a special sweat.

Sweat Lodge

The sweat lodge is an ancient purification ritual which was done in many native cultures. In the United States, most of the sweat lodges built and ceremonies conducted within the lodge reflect the Oglala Sioux tradition of the Inipi or Sweat Lodge, as recounted by Black Elk and told to Joseph Epes Brown in *The Sacred Pipe*. The sweat lodge incorporates the powers of the four elements: water, which is felt through the steam coming up from the rocks; earth, symbolized by the stones from Grandmother Earth; fire, the hot fire that heats the rocks; and air, which enters through the open door of the lodge. The young willows, from which the lodge is constructed, symbolize rebirth, because they come to life again in the spring, after dying and shedding their leaves in the fall.

The sweat lodge is constructed from twelve to sixteen young willows. It is helpful to have someone who has built a lodge previously assist in its construction; the gathering of these willows and the scraping and preparation of them allows one to get in touch with the new energy and to experience the earth's renewal. After the willows are bent and the structure of the lodge formed, blankets and heavy cloth are spread on the outside to keep out the light and retain the warmth of the fire. Rocks must also be gathered and brought to the place where the sweat lodge has

been built. The rocks must be of a certain size and type—volcanic—so they will withstand the intense heat of the fire.

Each time a sweat is performed, a sacred fire needs to be made for heating the rocks. The fire is made in a sacred fireplace a short distance from the lodge. This sacred fireplace is connected to the lodge by a sacred path; the path goes from the fire pit inside the lodge to a mound of dirt, known as the Grandmother Mound, on which sacred pipes and other ceremonial objects are placed. Just beyond the Grandmother Mound is the sacred fire.

To start a sacred fire, four bundles of eight twigs each are placed in tipi fashion in the center. The eight twigs are for each of the eight directions. On top of these are placed the wood and paper and the rocks to be heated for the sweat. It is important to have someone assist the group the first time this is done.

The rocks take several hours to heat up and during this time each woman can make special tobacco prayer bundles with cloth and tobacco. These are then tied together and strung around the lodge. Afterward they are burned so that all the prayers go up in smoke.

Colors are chosen for the prayer bundles, one representing each direction. Yellow is often used for the east, red for the south, black for the west, white for the north, green for Earth Mother, and blue for Sky

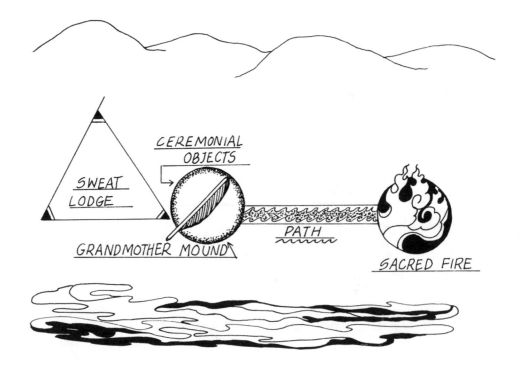

Father. Every woman makes four bundles for each direction making a total of twenty-four, or eight bundles for each direction, making a total of forty-eight. As she ties the tobacco bundle, she makes a prayer relating to that direction. This is a good meditative way to prepare for the sweat itself.

When the rocks are heated, everyone takes off all clothing and jewelry. Wearing a sheet or large towel inside the lodge is often helpful to absorb the body's sweat. Rattles are often taken into the lodge to use for chanting. Ceremonial objects and jewelry can be placed on the Grandmother Mound. One person is usually chosen as firekeeper; she will then bring in the rocks on a shovel before she joins the lodge. This position can be shared with a different woman doing each of the four rounds.

The person conducting the sweat sits on the end next to the bucket of water and dipper. When all the rocks are in, she splashes some water on the rocks so that they steam. Then she puts pinches of sage and cedar on the rocks and blesses them. This is done at the beginning of each round. There are usually four rounds, one for each direction.

The first round is for the east or air. The eagle who symbolizes east may be called in as well as any goddesses whose energy feels appropriate (Ix Chel, the Mayan moon goddess, who is connected with the eagle, is one. See the Invocation to Ix Chel in Chapter 2.) Each woman greets the stone people and tells of her intention for the sweat. Songs are sung to honor the east. These include "May We All Fly Like Eagles," "Spirit of the Wind," "The Return," "Wearing My Long Winged Feathers." (Any songs not given in previous chapters will be given at the end of this section.)

The second round is for the south. Here is where we open up to our passions and deep emotions, the heat and intensity that we feel. We may invoke any of the fire goddesses—Pele, Kali, Oya, Hestia, or Vesta. Each woman shares her deepest passions and explains the areas where she wants to open up more. Songs for the south may include "We All Come from the Goddess" (with the second stanza, We all come from the Sun God), "Wild Woman," and "Open My Heart."

West, the place of deep introspection, visions, and the home of the black bear is the next round. West is the place of change, so we may call in Changing Woman, Hecate, Inanna, or Persephone. Here we may share our deepest fears and what we need to do to move

farther in exploring our own inner depths. The west is the direction of water, so many of the songs that we share are related to the purifying energy of water. Songs include "The River," "Changing Woman," "Hina May" (the Bear Song), and "I Sing the Spirit."

North, the land of the buffalo and the ancients, is the fourth round of the sweat. In the north we attune to the grandmothers and grandfathers and listen to the wisdom they bring. We invoke White Buffalo Woman and her pipe. If there is a pipe to be smoked, it may be done in the north. (It may also be done in the west or any of the other rounds.) Each woman shares the wisdom she is seeking from the ancient ones. Songs to celebrate the north include "We Are the Old People," "Ancient Mother," "The Earth Is Our Mother," and "White Buffalo Woman."

In between each round the door is opened; water is brought in; and each woman drinks a bit, offering it first to Earth Mother, and then splashes herself with it. Some leaders allow women to leave the lodge in between rounds if they need to; others prefer that they stay inside. After the sweat, one jumps into water, such as a river or stream if it is near, or just an outdoor hose or shower. Then there is feasting and celebration.

Chants

The Return
The earth, the water, the fire, the air,
Return, return, return, return.

(Repeat first two lines)

He ya ya ya ya ya ya ya,
He yo yo yo yo yo yo yo.

(Repeat these two lines)[21]

I Sing the Spirit
I Sing the Spirit,
and the Spirit sings me,
It flows like a river,
and it flows through me.

(Make up new verses by changing the words,
as for example:
I sing the Wind,
I sing the Bird,
I sing the Moon,
I sing the Goddess, etc.)

White Buffalo Woman

White Buffalo Woman, I seek thy vision.
White Buffalo Woman, I seek thy grace.
White Buffalo Woman, I seek thy wisdom.
White Buffalo Woman, I seek thy peace.
Fill me with thy vision, fill me with thy grace,
Fill me with thy wisdom, fill me with thy peace.

(Tape: Lisa Theil, *Songs of the Spirit*)

If the sweat is performed in the night, the morning ceremony will involve prayers around the fire with tobacco, as was done on the Winter Solstice. Each woman prays for what she wants this new season to bring and for her own creative energy. She also makes prayers for any relatives or friends not present. The rest of the ceremony may deal with fertility, planting seeds, and talking about woman's fertility, puberty ceremonies, and how we each need to enhance our creative nature at this time.

Spring Equinox is also a joyful, playful time; it is the time of the young girl. Singing and dancing which allow the girl child to come out are important. After the morning ceremony, it is good to break the fast, and share spring vegetables and herbs along with traditional corn bread.

Beltane or May Day

Beltane was another of the ancient fire festivals in Europe. The name derives from the Celtic god Belenus, though not much is known of him. The Beltane fires and the Maypole celebrate fertility and the earth's ripe abundance. Persephone comes of age and is ready to experience her sexuality. Lovers sleep outdoors and copulate in the fields to insure the fertility of the crops. Dances are done around the Maypole during the day, and at night lovers jump over the Beltane fires and declare their intention to marry at the Midsummer Solstice.

Another tradition at this time in Germany was that of Walpurgisnacht or Walpurgis Night, the night before May Day. This night was considered similar to Hallowe'en in that witches or spirits of the dead were said to be everywhere. The kindling of fires on Walpurgis Night was to drive away the witches.[22]

Beltane is the time of the sacred marriage; the Goddess and God were known as the Queen and King of the May. Originally the Goddess was portrayed as Diana, or Artemis, Queen of the Wood, and her consort, Virbius. Many countries had ceremonies where a human married the image of a goddess or god at this time. All these rites were to insure the fertility of nature, just as the fires were purificatory and were believed to protect against pestilence, plague, and epidemics.

May Day is a time when each of us needs to perform her own sacred marriage, the union of our female and male selves. Once our female and male sides are in balance, we can walk in balance in the outside world. Often our male sides push us to accomplish tasks and make ourselves heard in the world, while our female parts desire to stay home, nurture our bodies, be outside in nature, listen to music and poetry. We need to be aware of both these voices and to connect with our individual female and male selves. The Huna work from Hawaii provides a wonderful tool for doing this. In the Huna work, we learn to communicate with our Higher Self and then our female and male basic selves. Through having the three parts speak with each other, we understand the nature of our problems and the relationship between our female and male.

Ritual

The first part of the ritual is to decorate a tree or pole for a Maypole which is the fertility totem. A pole can be stuck into the earth, after a hole about one foot deep has been dug. The base can be steadied with rocks. Women bring colored streamers, fresh flowers, and spring herbs to weave around this pole. As women weave these beautiful female plants around the male symbol, they should be aware that they are balancing their own (lunar and solar) energies.

The Maypole becomes the center of the circle during the ritual. On the ground around the Maypole are rose and red candles; roses and other fragrant flowers; and ripe fruits, such as cherries and strawberries, to symbolize fertility. Also use objects to designate the four directions as a feather, candle, water, and cornmeal. Pictures of fertility goddesses such as Aphrodite, Isis, Venus, Ishtar, Asherah, Cybele, and Freya are also appropriate.

The High Priestess calls in the four directions by invoking particular goddesses and also the god or Sky Father to complete the sacred marriage.

Each woman shares prayers for the fertility of spring and asks to balance her own lunar and solar sides. Chants are intoned as dancers circle the Maypole. Later there is feasting on sensual foods such as berries and cream, cherry cobbler, and colorful fresh spring vegetables.

In the evening a sacred fire is built and each woman sacrifices to the fire something she wants to give up in order to bring her female and male selves into balance. If there are men present at the ritual, they too, sacrifice something to the fire. The leader or High Priestess speaks about the balance in nature reflecting the balance in each of us. Chanting and drumming are done around the fire.

Chants for Beltane

We Are the Flow (*Shekinah Mountain Water*)
(*may be sung while weaving the Maypole*)
We are the flow, We are the ebb,
We are the weaver, We are the web.[23]

We All Come from the Goddess
We all come from the Goddess,
And to her we shall return.
Like a drop of rain,
Flowing to the ocean.

We all come from the Sun God,
And to him we shall return.
Like a spark of flame,
Floating to the heavens.[24]

(Tape: *From the Goddess—*
On Wings of Song,
Robert Gass)

We Are the Dance of the Moon and the Sun
We are the dance of the moon and the sun,
We are the power in everyone,
We are the hope that will not hide.
We are the turning of the tide.[25]

Summer Solstice

As the light of the sun increases, we approach the time of the Summer Solstice or Midsummer's Eve, the longest day of the year. This is a time when the sun reaches its zenith, appears to stand still for a few days, and then turns southward. It is a time to unleash the dark forces within us and to prepare for the waning of the sun's power. To the Native Americans, this was not as strong a time as the Winter Solstice, but their ceremonies do include a four-day fast and prayers to entreat the sun to get back on its course. In Europe, Midsummer's Eve was the strongest of the fire festi-

vals. Fires were kept burning all night with singing, dancing, drinking of mead and ale, and lovemaking in the fields. One European custom at this time was to roll a burning wheel down a hillside to imitate the action of the sun and for purification of any evil spirits. In Europe these festivals became associated with St. John's Day (June 24) and were often done the evening before. St. Johnswort is a sacred herb associated with the Summer Solstice just as mistletoe is used at the Winter Solstice. St. Johnswort is often put under the pillow to increase psychic sensitivity; from the herb is made a deep red oil that is helpful for cuts, bruises, and other wounds.

In the Demeter/Persephone myth, Persephone, who has come of age at Beltane, enters the labyrinth leading to Hecate and the underworld at Summer Solstice. Demeter does not learn of her entrance until the Fall Equinox when she grieves for Persephone and all the vegetation dies. But now, at Summer Solstice, there is just the beginning of darkness. As the sun starts to wane, we all look at the darkness embedded within.

Ritual

Midsummer's Eve, the night before the solstice, is a good time for a moon ceremony. The ceremony is similar to that done on Winter Solstice; the moon altar faces east as in winter, but in spring and fall it faces west. On the moon altar may be red and yellow candles, symbolic of the sun's heat, red flowers as roses and other summer flowers, St. Johnswort and the red oil made from it. There also may be pictures of the fire goddesses such as Pele, Kali, Oya, as well as goddesses of sexuality and fertility such as Aphrodite, Ishtar, Astarte, Tiamat, and Yemaya. A sacred fire is built, and after the moon ceremony, a spiral dance may be done around the fire.

The High Priestess or leader conducts the spiral dance, beginning in a clockwise direction, taking the line of women around the land, then back to the fire. The beginning of the chain of women is wound in on itself so that the women are bound together. Then the High Priestess unravels this chain, moving outward in the opposite direction. The line snakes around the land again, and when it returns to the fire, each woman, one by one, leaves the chain and walks to the fire with some special wish she wants at this time and something she will release into the fire. When all have put their wishes and sacrifices into the fire, chants are sung, and the women dance around the fire, embracing the lushness of the season and remembering the beginning of darkness approaching. The circle is closed and beverages may be shared.

The following morning sunrise ceremony is done, with each woman receiving a pinch of tobacco to make prayers for the new season. After each one puts her tobacco into the fire, the welcome song is sung (see Winter Solstice, "Hey Ungula"). Then the fast is broken with summer fruits, seeds and nuts, and corn bread.

Chants for Summer Solstice

May the Long Time Sun

May the long time sun shine upon you,
All love surround you,
And the pure light within you,
Guide your way home.[26]

(Robert Williamson, Lyrics)

Let Me Be One with the Infinite Sun

Let me be one with the Infinite Sun
Forever and ever and ever.
(Repeat)
Ku-wa-te le-no le-no
Ma ho te
Aya no aya no aya no
(Repeat)[27]

Lammas, August 1

Lammas, or Lughnasadh (after the Celtic God Lugus) is one of the harvest festivals. It is a time of corn dances for the green corn. In the Hopi tradition, the Snake-Antelope dance is held every other year. At certain pueblos, including Santo Domingo in New Mexico, the annual corn dance is held around this time.

In the Persephone/Demeter cycle, Persephone reaches Hecate in the underground. Demeter is just beginning to realize that Persephone is gone. Inanna has also entered the underworld and has begun her pilgrimage to visit her sister Ereshkigal. The descent into the dark has just begun; the lushness of summer is still evident, and gardens are full of summer greens and late summer crops as squashes, zucchini, and corn.

All cultures had representations of a corn mother or corn goddess. In Europe the corn mother was made of the last sheaves of corn harvested; her spirit was believed to be embodied in these sheaves of corn. The Mandans and Minnitarees of North America believed that a certain Old Woman Who Never Dies made the crops grow; in spring she sent various migratory birds as her representative to bring certain crops—the wild goose for maize, the wild swan for gourds, and the wild duck for beans.[28] The Native Americans left offerings to the Old Woman during the year. In the fall, when the birds started flying south, they thought that the birds were going home to the Old Woman, so they took offerings as dried meat to the older women in the tribe so that the game would not depart too soon, and the cold would not come too soon.[29]

It is this feeling for the corn mother, for the harvest, and for the beginnings of the cold and winter, that is experienced at the time of Lammas, just as in early morning walks in August, one experiences the feeling of fall in the air.

Ritual

The altar should be decorated with late summer herbs and plants—corn, zucchini, summer squash, grapes—as well as green, orange, and yellow candles. Goddess figurines and representations of the Earth Mother and corn mother should be placed around the altar. Some of these goddesses include Demeter, Ceres, Chicomecoatl (Aztec corn mother), Mawu (African earth mother), Kwan Yin, Gaia, and Spider Grandmother.

After smudging, call in the four directions. One of the corn goddesses may be called in for each direction:

To the East, I call in Kwan Yin, the Great Mother of the Orient and Eastern countries;
To the South, I call in Chicomecoatl, Corn Mother of the southern countries, and provider for us;
To the West, I call in Ceres, who brings us grain and nurture;
To the North, I call in Spider Grandmother, for her wisdom and foresight;
I call in Earth Mother for her nurture;
And I call in Sky Father for his guidance.

Each woman then shares how she will harvest her ideas in the fall, what she will do during the dark cycle, how she will face her inner fears. Each woman may make an offering to the fire, if there is one. Afterwards there is chanting and dancing; women partake of corn bread (the transformation of the corn) and wine or grape juice (the transformation of the grapes). Harvest songs and dances are shared.

Chants

May You Walk in Beauty
May you walk in beauty
In a sacred way.
May you walk in beauty
Each and every day.
(Repeat)
May the beauty of the air,
Help your mind see clearer.
May the beauty of the fire,
Reach your heart's desire.
May the beauty of the water,
Flow to sons and daughters.
May the beauty of the earth,
Bring you laughter and mirth.
(Repeat first four lines.)

Fall Equinox

This time of equal day and equal night marks the beginning of the death of Grandfather Sun; it is a time to gather the harvest and reap what we have sown in the spring. The abundance of the harvest is present, but so is our sense of preparation for the dark, cold winter and the death of nature. Fall Equinox is the time Demeter mourns for Persephone and thus causes all in the natural world to die and mourn with her. In other goddess cultures Astarte mourned Adonis (Syria), Cybele mourned Attis (Phrygia), and Isis mourned Osiris (Egypt). It is a time of going within ourselves and making preparations for our survival, physically and spiritually, during the winter months. In terms of directions, fall is west, the home of the black bear, the time for introspection and deep thought.

For many thousands of years in Greek culture, the Eleusinian Mysteries were celebrated at the Fall Equinox. The Eleusinian Mysteries dealt with the mystery of life and death and involved nine days of ceremonies. One of the bases of the Mysteries is that Demeter transforms the barren, brown land of the Eleusinian plain into a field of golden grain. In the Mysteries, one ear of corn was shown to the participants to illustrate that each birth was the coming back of the soul and that the earth's cycle of birth and death reflected the human cycle.

Ritual

The night prior to the equinox, it is good to have a sweat. In the darkness of the sweat lodge, each woman is able to face her own darkness, her fears for the winter and the coming cycle. (The sweat lodge should face west at this time, if possible, since the issues we are dealing with are those of the west.)

The following morning, before sunrise, one woman makes the sacred fire. Around the fire are placed harvest foods—corn and squash, pumpkins, gourds of all types; fall flowers such as marigolds; and candles of orange, gold, and yellow. In the middle one black candle may be placed to symbolize the approaching darkness.

At sunrise, the woman or High Priestess who is conducting the ceremony gives each woman a pinch of tobacco with which to say her prayers. She, along with other women, invokes the four directions with some of the goddesses.

To the East I call in Gaia, the Great Earth Mother,
To the South, I call in Pele, goddess of fire and purification,
To the West, I call in Inanna, she who sees and understands the dark,
To the North, I call in White Buffalo Woman, who brings us the wisdom of the Ancients (or Spider Grandmother).
I call in the Earth Mother,
And the Sky Father.

As each woman goes to the fire with her tobacco, she prays for the new season, asking for what she needs at this time. She also prays for the earth and any relatives or friends that are not present. (Red tobacco bundles, made beforehand, are used for those not present and then thrown into the fire.)

The greeting song is then sung ("Hey Ungula"); other chants are shared as well as prayers for balance and peace, since this is the time of the balance of the light and dark. When the ceremony is over, the fast is broken with corn bread, freshly harvested vegetables as baked squash and pumpkins, and fall fruits.

Chants

Changing Woman (Adele Getty)
She changes everything she touches,
And everything she touches, changes,
Changing woman, rearranges,

Changing woman, rearranges.
Change us, touch us, touch us, change us.
Everything lost is found again, in a new form, in a
   new way.
Everything hurt is healed again, in a new life, in a
   new day.[30]

She Will Bring

For she will bring the buds in the spring,
And laugh among the flowers.
In summer's heat her kisses are sweet,
She sings in leafy bowers.
She cuts the cane and gathers the grain,
When the fruits of fall surround her.
Her bones grow old and wintery cold,
She wraps her cloak around her.

For he will call the leaves in fall,
To fly their colors brightly.
When warmth is lost he paints with frost,
His silver touches lightly.
He greets the day of the dance in May,
His ribbons round about him.
We eat the corn and drink from his horn,
We would not be without him.

All Hallows, October 31

Hallows, All Hallows Eve, Samhain, are names for the celebration that marks the end of the year and the beginning of the new cycle. This is a time when the veil between the living and dead is very thin; it is a time when we can communicate with the spirits of the ancestors and the recently departed. It is the time of transition from autumn to winter, when the spirits of the departed come back, seeking their warm homes for the next season. In the Demeter/Persephone myth, it represents the time when Demeter finds Persephone in the underworld and begins the long journey back with Persephone in her womb, to be born again at the Winter Solstice.

Hallows was one of the ancient fire festivals from old Europe. In Scotland, on the last day of autumn, children gathered ferns and long thin stalks and placed them near the house. In the evening, these were set on fire; each house had its fire (these fires were called *Samhnagan*).[31] As in the Beltane fires, the purpose of these fires was for purification, not only physical purification, but also for dispersing negative spirits (which were referred to as "witches"). In ancient Ireland, a new fire was kindled every year on All Hallows Eve, and from this sacred flame, all the fires in Ireland were rekindled.[32]

Hallowe'en is the time of the crone, the wise woman, and the honoring of the crone goddesses from many cultures. These goddesses include Hecate (Greece), Kali (India), Cerridwyn (Wales), Oya (Africa), Inanna and Ereshkigal (Sumer), Nepthys (Egypt), Sedna (Inuit), Copper Woman and Spider Grandmother (Native American), Baba Yaga (Russia), the Morrigan (Ireland), Hella (Scandinavia), and Holla (Germany). The cauldron of the crone is usually used in the center of the circle for rituals. The cauldron comes from the legend of Cerridwyn who had a magic cauldron. The nine women who guarded this magic cauldron may have been Druid priestesses from the island of Sein off the coast of Brittany; these women could impersonate animal spirits.[33]

Many animal spirits are present at this time and speak through the witches or wise women. The custom of wearing costumes arose so mortals could impersonate these animal spirits and the spirits of the dead to bring them back to life. Many cultures invoke the spirits of departed ancestors at Hallowe'en; in Mexico this time is referred to as "El Dia de las Muertes" (the Day of the Dead) and ceremonies last a whole week. The ceremony is dedicated to the Aztec goddess Tonantzin, who later was worshipped as the Virgin of Guadalupe. The Christian world celebrates at this time and calls it All Saints' Day.

Hallows is a good time for looking into the future through the use of scrying and crystal balls; it is also an important time for getting rid of old habits and patterns. The fire in the cauldron should be used for burning and banishing the old. Prayers are also made for departed ones, for ancestors and those we want to remember as the many wise women who were burned in Europe as witches.

Ritual

A sacred fire is made in the cauldron in the center of the circle. On the altar are placed black candles, owl's wings (the owl is a bird of the night and is associated with the dead, also with the wise women and with magic), pumpkins with candles in them, skulls of animals and birds, pictures of the crone goddesses, and pomegranates (which will be used in the ceremony).

Women are dressed in costume and with masks of the goddess or ancestor or animal spirit they are impersonating. There is an eerie atmosphere with cackling and high voices of the crones. After all are smudged, the leader or High Priestess calls in the four directions:

> To the East, we call in Hecate, Crone Goddess of the Dark Moon. Bring in all those spirits that we need to communicate with tonight.
> To the South, we call in Kali, creatress and destructress. Purify us with your fire.
> To the West, we call in Inanna. Return from the underworld and teach us how to enter that dark space.
> To the North, we call in Spider Grandmother. Bring us the wisdom from the ancient grandmother circle.

Women form a line and snake their way around the circle chanting "Isis, Astarte, Diana, Hecate, Demeter, Kali, Inanna." They then begin a spiral dance moving toward the cauldron at the center. The movement is counterclockwise to suggest the old cycle and banishing the old. Each woman walks up to the fire and throws in a piece of paper on which she has written something; she then shouts out what it is she is letting go of, "I banish my fear," etc. Then the spiral dance is done again; this time clockwise to indicate the new cycle.

When all have returned to their place in the circle, one woman dressed as a crone goddess walks up to them with a plate containing pieces of pomegranate. She tells them to take a piece only if they agree to return to the underground. When this is completed, there is chanting, drumming, and dancing around the fire. Later, women may present a poem or dance expressing the goddess they are impersonating. Autumn foods such as hot cider, baked squash, and pumpkin pie may be shared.

Chants

(This song may be sung by someone who knows it or the tape played. It is from the tape *Catch the Fire* by Charlie Murphy, produced by Art Front Music, P.O. Box 12188, Seattle, WA 98102.)

Burning Times

In the cool of the evening they used to gather
'Neath stars in the meadow circled near an old oak tree,
At the times appointed by the seasons of the earth
And the phases of the moon.
In the center often stood a woman, equal with the others,
And respected for her worth.
One of the many we call the witches,
The healers and the teachers of the wisdom of the earth.
The people grew through the knowledge she gave them—
Herbs to heal their bodies,
Spells to make their spirits whole.
Hear them chanting healing incantations,
Calling forth the wise ones,
Celebrating in dance and song.

Chorus (*by Deena Metzger*)

Isis, Astarte, Diana, Hecate,
Demeter, Kali, Inanna.

There were those who came to power through domination
And they bonded in their worship
Of a dead man on a cross.
They sought control of the common people
By demanding allegiance to the Church of Rome.
And the Pope declared the Inquisition.
It was a war against the women whose powers he had feared.
In this holocaust against the nature people
Nine million European women died.
And the tale is told of those who by the hundreds
Holding together chose their death in the sea.
While chanting the praises of the Mother Goddess
A refusal of betrayal—
Women were dying to be free.

Chorus

Now the Earth is a witch and the men still burn her,
Stripping her down with mining and the poisons of their wars.

But to us the Earth is a healer, a teacher, our
 mother,
The weaver of the web of life that keeps us all alive.
She gives us the vision to see through the chaos,
She gives us the courage, it is our will to survive.

The Song of the Ancestors

Chorus

Listen more often to things than to beings.
Listen more often to things than to beings.
Tis the Ancestors word when the fire's voice is
 heard.
Tis the Ancestors word in the voice of the water.

Those who have died have never, never, left;
The dead are not under the Earth.
They are in the rustling leaves,
They are in the groaning wood,
They are in the crying grass,
The dead are not under the Earth.

Chorus

Those who have died have never, never, left
The dead have a pact with the living.
They are in the woman's breast,
The are in the waiting child,
They are with us in the home,
They are with us in the ground,
The dead have a pact with the living.

Chorus

(Tape: *Good News*,
Sweet Honey in the Rock)

Sacred Ancestors

Sacred ancestors come to me,
Sacred ancestors who love me,

Sacred ancestors come to me,
Sacred ancestors, please help me.

All my mothers, fathers, sisters, brothers,
and relations too,
Who have loved me for always,
I keep the light for you.

(Tape: *Prayers for the Planet*,
Lisa Thiel)

Who Were the Witches?

Chorus

Who were the witches?
Where did they come from?
Maybe your great-great-grandmother was one.
Witches were wise, wise women they say,
And there's a little witch in every woman today.

Witches knew all about flowers and weeds,
How to use all of their roots and their seeds.
When people grew weary from hard-working days,
They made them feel better in so many ways.

Chorus

When women had babies, the witches were there,
To help them and hold them and give them sweet
 care.
Witches knew stories about how life began,
Do you wish you could be one? Well, maybe you
 can.

Chorus

Some people thought that the witches were bad,
Some people feared all the power they had.
But the power to help and to heal and to cure
Is nothing to fear, it is something to share.

Chorus

(Tape: *Songs to the Goddess*,
Sonoma County Birth Network)

ENDNOTES

1. Williamson, Ray, *Living the Sky: The Cosmos of the American Indian*, p. 38.
2. *Ibid.*, p. 39.
3. *Ibid.*, p. 40.
4. *Ibid.*, p. 106.
5. *Ibid.*, p. 110.
6. *Ibid.*, p. 114.
7. *Ibid.*, p. 201.
8. Eddy, John, A., "Astronomical Alignment of the Big Horn Medicine Wheel," in *Science*, 184, 1974.
9. Graves, Robert, *The White Goddess*, New York, Farrar, Straus & Giroux, 1981, pp. 165–166.
10. Williamson, p. 282.
11. *Ibid.*
12. *Ibid.*, pp. 283–285.
13. Fewkes, J. Walter, "A Few Summer Ceremonials at the Tusayan Pueblos," *Journal of American Ethnology and Archaeology* 2, 1892, p. 27.
14. Stephen, Alexander, M., *Hopi Journal of Alexander Stephen*, ed. by E.C. Parsons, Columbia University Contributions to Anthropology 23, New York, 1936.
15. Stevenson, Matilda Cox, "The Zuni Indians," Smithsonian Institution, *Bureau of American Ethnology Annual Report* 23, 1904.
16. Kealoha, p. 94.
17. *Ibid.*, p. 138.
18. Stone, Merlin, *Ancient Mirrors of Womanhood*, p. 64.
19. *Ibid.*
20. Kealoha, p. 143.
21. *Ibid.*, p. 118.
22. Frazer, p. 720.
23. Kealoha, p. 175.
24. *Ibid.*, p. 169.
25. *Ibid.*, p. 172.
26. *Ibid.*, p. 144.
27. *Ibid.*, p. 102.
28. Frazer, p. 486.
29. *Ibid.*, p. 487.
30. Kealoha, p. 176.
31. Frazer, p. 735.
32. *Ibid.*, p. 234.
33. Stone, Merlin, *Ancient Mirrors of Womanhood*, p. 59.

Performing
Women's Medicine Ways
Ceremonies

I am at a large women's solstice camp in the mountains of New Mexico. Women of many ethnic backgrounds are in attendance. At one of the evening circles the women are singing "Amazing Grace." As I look into the eyes of each woman in this circle, I see the love she holds for her sisters and the bonding between all the women. I also see something larger than the individuals composing this circle. I see an energy and a power that goes beyond words. It is the Great Mystery, the Goddess, Gaia herself—a force that is capable of creating significant changes on the planet through the power of feminine love and connection. This is the force that the Palestinian and Israeli women feel when they come together; they know that if, as women, they can forge strong bonds, they may, in time, be able to heal the deep wounds between their two nations. They know they may end the hate and bigotry that exist in most of their political leaders, leaders who know only the way of the sword and the intellect. This is the power that we seek as women—the power to change and heal the existing patriarchal structure which works to dominate, possess, and have power over both the environment and other individuals.

Sometimes women need to begin slowly, in smaller, more personal rituals and ceremonies so that they can heal themselves before attempting to reach out to larger social and political causes. For many women, their healing needs to go back to puberty—that time when they first felt the pain and the wonder of their femininity. I often guide women on a journey back to the time of their puberty so they can experience a ceremony or ritual for the beginning of womanhood. This ceremony enables them to erase old negative pictures and habits in order to begin anew. I have worked with several women who experienced deep change in their lives after participating in this ceremony where they could become the beautiful, powerful female whose being they felt was denied to them previously. One woman gave up her job as a teacher and allowed herself to work as an artist as she always had desired. Her parents had discouraged her by telling her she would never be able to support herself and that art was totally impractical.

Another extremely important ceremony is birthing. How many of us have reexperienced our own birth—either formally with rebirthing techniques, or informally by feeling again the pain and trauma of being pulled from the womb by forceps or simply pushed, shoved, and forced out into a foreign environment while our mothers were often so sedated they weren't awake to greet us. Many of us have come to dislike the medical profession because of that initial welcome; we have even felt betrayed by our own mothers. Fortunately, today there is a rising interest in natural childbirth, birthing at home with the help of a midwife, or having the baby "room in" in the hospital to allow the parents to interact with the new family member in a loving, caring way. I have worked with several women who gave birth by Caesarean section that still feel angry about it. Going back and redoing the experience in a natural way has helped alleviate their anger. It is also important that their children go through a natural birth because often the children are still traumatized by their birth. Working in ritual together, redoing the birth experience has proved extremely helpful for several mothers and children I know. A stronger bonding has resulted and tensions between mother and child have eased considerably.

Preparing ritually for a birth can be helpful to siblings of the new baby. They have the opportunity to participate in the birth process by creating a birthing altar, praying, and feeling in tune with their mother as she goes through labor. This is especially true for younger children who may become frightened at their mother's screams and feel something bad is happening to her. At one birth I attended, I brought the young daughter a ritual dress to wear, and we created an altar and performed chants while the mother was in labor. Including the siblings and the father in the birth process provides a stronger family bonding.

Marriage and partnership ceremonies often create permanent wounds because many women sacrifice their wishes to the demands of their families regarding the type and location of the ceremony. They then have negative memories of their marriage day because they weren't performing a ritual that expressed their own individuality. Often, they didn't know what they wanted at the time. Finally, years later, they can recreate the ceremony in a way that expresses their own beliefs and values. This is often a good time for the partners to recommit to their relationship. Ongoing ceremonies to celebrate different stages of a relationship are appropriate; it doesn't have to be a calendar anniversary to do this.

Many women at menopause come to view ritual with new eyes. The easing of daily responsibilities allows them time to think about this new phase and what it means. The biological changes, which are gradual, have a way of preparing them for the important rite of passage and the significance of the "change of life." As teenagers, we were so caught up in our lives that we never spent much time thinking about puberty (unless we grew up in a native culture where rituals were traditional, or some adult took time to prepare a puberty rite for us). We now have the wisdom and understanding to make this biological transition a meaningful one. So many women start out having to overcome the negative press on menopause and incorrect information on the aging process, the push to use estrogen replacement therapy, and the fear of osteoporosis and other ailments. They forget the beauty and wisdom inherent in this phase until they bond with other women and, through ritual, empower themselves. Taking on a new name, beginning some new type of work or creative endeavor are all results of participating consciously in this rite. Often crone/grandmother circles are formed to continue the bonding and celebration that occurs at this time (certainly as a support group to discuss the problems of aging).

If we bond with other women at menopause, it is easier to face the time when our friends and relatives begin to cross over. We then have the ceremonial tools to work with and the sisterhood to call on for assistance. It is never easy to prepare someone for crossing over or to conduct a ceremony for one's relatives and friends after they have passed on. Many years ago, in the early '70s, a young girl I knew (she was my astrology student and rented a room in the home of one of my friends) committed suicide by shooting herself. She was just twenty-one, intelligent and talented, but she suffered periods of depression and confusion. No one, of course, realized how deep her depression was, least of all her family (she had a younger sister and brother in addition to her parents). I organized a ceremony for her parents, siblings, and friends. Everyone shared how they felt about her and what they would miss about her. There were lots of tears and a lot of love. A few of us read poems and statements about crossing over. We were all beginners on the spiritual path then, and we sought metaphysically to understand this death which seemed so violent and so premature. Sharing and bonding through ritual was beautiful and very helpful to the girl's family. I have had to thank her spirit again and again for teaching us the power of such rituals. Since that time I have given or participated in others—each one as different as the personalities we celebrated and grieved for. But always there was the feeling that by our bonding we were keeping alive the spirit of the particular friend who had departed. By being together we could console and support each other in our loss.

As we journey through the realm of the many mysteries and medicine ways that we as women share, we live each day from dawn till dusk celebrating the movement of the sun. We live each month from new moon to full moon watching the movement of the moon across the night sky. In yearly rituals we commemorate the seasons and the earth's turning. For each of us to follow these daily, monthly, and yearly cycles is to acknowledge our own inner rhythms and to prepare for our larger life cycles as they unfold. To stay attuned to nature is to become aware of our own cycles as we move forward on our earth walk.

May we dance in beauty with our mother Gaia; may we unite with all women to create a strong sisterhood.

Appendix

Four Directions

East

Time of Day—dawn
Season—spring
Element—air
Animal—eagle, hawk, deer
Plants—Trees—ash, aspen, birch, beech; gold and
    yellow flowers
Minerals—topaz, jasper, citrine quartz
Incenses—lavender, lemon balm
Goddesses—Spider Woman (Native American),
    Athena (Greece), Lilith (Hebrew), Aido Hwedo
    (Haiti)

West

Time of Day—dusk, sunset
Season—autumn
Element—water
Animal—bear, jaguar, panther, snake, owl, raven
Plants—Trees—willow; blue and purple flowers
Minerals—smoky quartz, black onyx, obsidian, moon-
    stone, opal, pearl
Incenses—sage, myrrh, sandalwood, mugwhort
Goddesses—Changing Woman (Native American),
    Kali (India), Inanna/Ereshkigal (Sumeria),
    Medusa (African), Sekhmet (Egypt), Hecate
    (Greece), Cerridwyn (Wales)

South

Time of Day—noon, midday
Season—summer
Element—fire
Animal—coyote, mouse, fox, tiger, lion
Plants—Trees—maple; red and orange flowers
Minerals—carnelian, garnet, ruby, bloodstone
Incenses—juniper, frankincense, cedar
Goddesses—Pele (Hawaii), Hestia (Greece), Vesta
    (Rome), Sun Woman (Native American), Oya
    (Africa), Amaterasu (Japan)

North

Time of Day—night
Season—winter
Element—earth
Animal—buffalo, moose, wolf
Plants—Trees—oak, redwood, pine, eucalyptus; all
    green herbs
Minerals—turquoise, chrysocolla, malachite, emerald
Incenses—pine, cedar
Goddesses—White Buffalo Woman (Native Ameri-
    can), Oshun (Africa), Demeter (Greece), Isis
    (Egypt), Ishtar (Middle East), Ceres (Rome)

Moon Phases

New Moon
- Moon is 0–45 degrees ahead of the sun.
- Moon rises at dawn, sets at sunset.
- Moon is from exact new moon to 3-1/2 days after.
- The seed or project is initiated; an instinctive time, energy is within.
- Winter Solstice, December 21.

Crescent
- Moon is 45–90 degrees ahead of the sun.
- Moon rises mid-morning, sets after sunset.
- Moon is 3-1/2 to 7 days after the new moon.
- The new seed is challenged to move forward; a time of struggle.
- Candlemas, February 2, the beginnings of spring are felt.

First Quarter
- Moon is 90–135 degrees ahead of the sun.
- Moon rises at noon, sets at midnight.
- Moon is from 7 to 10-1/2 days after the new moon.
- The new project takes form; a critical time as it establishes itself in its environment; a time of action.
- Spring Equinox, March 21.

Gibbous
- Moon is 135–180 degrees ahead of the sun.
- Moon rises in mid-afternoon, sets around 3 A.M.
- Moon is between 10-1/2 to 14 days after the new moon.
- A time to analyze the form of the seed or project; a time to perfect.
- Beltane, May 1.

Full Moon
- Moon is 180–225 degrees ahead of the sun.
- Moon rises at sunset, sets at dawn.
- Moon is from 14 to 17-1/2 days after the new moon.
- The illumination and full meaning of the project is revealed.
- Summer Solstice, June 21.

Disseminating
- Moon is 225–270 degrees ahead of the sun.
- Moon rises at mid-evening, sets at mid-morning.
- Moon is 3-1/2 to 7 days after the full moon.
- The meaning of the project or idea is disseminated or shared.
- Lammas, August 1.

Last Quarter
- Moon is 270–315 degrees ahead of the sun.
- Moon rises at midnight and sets at noon.
- Moon is 7 to 10-1/2 days after the full moon.
- The breakdown of form, dissolution.
- Fall Equinox, September 21.

Balsamic (Dark Moon)
- Moon is 315–360 degrees ahead of the sun.
- Moon rises at 3 A.M., sets mid-afternoon.
- Moon is 10-1/2 to 14 days after the full moon.
- The impulse for new forms comes from dreams.
- All Hallows, October 31.

Astrological Signs

Sign	Herbs	Gemstones	Aromas & Oils	Goddesses
Aries	nettle cayenne	carnelian bloodstone ruby	cinnamon clove	Pele Fuji Oya
Taurus	licorice anise	emerald malachite	rose jasmine bergamot	Aphrodite Venus Ishtar
Gemini	mullein coltsfoot	cat's eye tiger's eye	lavendar rosemary	Artemis Apollo Isis Osiris
Cancer	mugwhort hops	moonstone pearl opal	cypress juniper	Selene Diana Ix Chel
Leo	hawthorn borage	citrine topaz amber	orange patchouli	Sekhmet Brigit
Virgo	fennel papaya dill	earth-colored agates	peppermint thyme	Demeter Ceres Chicomecoatl
Libra	uva ursi dandelion leaf	chrysoprase aventurine	ylang ylang geranium	Athena Venus Aphrodite
Scorpio	ginseng squawvine chaste berry	smoky quartz obsidian	cedar sage melissa	Hecate Kali Medusa Lilith
Sagittarius	dandelion root chicory	turquoise chrysocola	sandalwood	Artemis Amazons
Capricorn	comfrey root comfrey leaf	diamond onyx	eucalyptus pine	Gaia Demeter Mujaji
Aquarius	vervain valerian catnip	lapis sapphire aquamarine amethyst	chamomile marjoram	Athena
Pisces	kelp dulse	coral flourite jade	myrrh frankincense	Kwan Yin Ala

Bibliography

Allen, Paula Gunn. *Grandmothers of the Light—A Medicine Woman's Sourcebook*. Boston, MA: Beacon Press, 1991.

Adler, Margot. *Drawing Down the Moon*. Boston, MA: Beacon Press, 1979.

Austen, Hallie Iglehart. *The Heart of the Goddess*. Berkeley, CA: Wingbow, 1990.

Bailey, Flora. "Same Sex Beliefs and Practices in Navajo Country." *Papers of Peabody Museum*. Cambridge, MA, Vol. 40:2, 1950.

Baker, Jeannine Parvati; Baker, Frederick; and Slayton, Tamara. *Conscious Conception—Elemental Journey through the Labyrinth of Sexuality*. Monroe, UT: Freestone Publishing, 1986.

Baker, Jeannine Parvati. *Hygeia—A Woman's Herbal*. Monroe, UT: Freestone Publishing, 1978.

Baker, Jeannine Parvati. *Pre-natal Yoga & Natural Birth*. Monroe, UT: Freestone Publishing, 1982.

Barnes, Alfred. *Mandan Social and Ceremonial Organization*. Chicago, IL: Univ.of Chicago Press, 1950.

Basso, Keith. "The Gift of Changing Woman," *Bureau of American Ethnology Papers*. Washington, DC: Smithsonian Institute, 1966.

Basso, Keith. *Girl's Puberty Ceremony*. NY: Holt, Rhinehart, & Winston, 1928.

Beck, Peggy V., and Walters, Anna L. *The Sacred—Ways of Knowledge, Sources of Life*. Tsaile, AZ: Navajo Community College Press, 1984.

Bierhorst, John, ed. *In the Trail of the Wind—American Indian Poems and Ritual Orations*. NY: Farrar, Straus, & Giroux, 1971.

Bolen, Jean Shinoda, M.D. *Goddesses in Everywoman*. NY: Harper & Row, 1984.

Brown, Joseph Epes, ed. *The Sacred Pipe: Black Elk's Account of the Seven Rites of the Oglala Sioux*. Norman, OK: University of Oklahoma, 1953.

Budapest, Z. *The Holy Book of Women's Mysteries, Part I & II*. Berkeley, CA: Susan B. Anthony Books, 1980.

Budapest, Z. *The Grandmother of Time*. San Francisco, CA: Harper & Row, 1989.

Bunzel, Ruth. "Zuni Origin Myths." *Bureau of American Ethnology Papers*. Washington, DC: Smithsonian Institute, 1932.

Crow Dog, Mary. *Lakota Woman*. San Francisco, CA: Harper & Collins, 1990.

Daly, Mary. *Gyn/Ecology*. Boston, MA: Beacon, 1990.

Doreal, tr. *The Emerald Tablets of Thoth the Atlantean*. Sedalia, CO: Brotherhood of the White Temple, 1939.

Eaton, Evelyn, *I Send a Voice*. Wheaton, IL: Theosophical Publishing House, 1978.

Eaton, Evelyn, *The Shaman and the Medicine Wheel*. Wheaton, IL: Theosophical Publishing House, 1982.

Eddy, John A. "Astronomical Alignment of the Big Horn Medicine Wheel," *Science* 184 (1974) pp.1035-43.

Farrar, Stewart. *Eight Sabbats for Witches*. Custer, WA: Phoenix Publishing, 1981.

Fewkes, Jesse W. "A Few Summer Ceremonials at the Tusayan Pueblos." *Journal of American Ethnology and Archaeology*, 1892.

Fletcher, Alice C., and La Flesche, Francis. *The Omaha Tribe*. Bureau of American Ethnology Papers, Washington, DC: Smithsonian Institute, 1911.

Frazer, Sir James G. *The Golden Bough*. NY: Macmillan, 1960.

Frisbee, Charlotte. *Kinaalda—A Study of the Navajo Girl's Puberty Ceremony*. Middletown, CT: Wesleyan University Press, 1967.

Gadon, Elinor W. *The Once & Future Goddess*. San Francisco, CA: Harper & Row, 1989.

Gaskell, Mrs. *Charlotte Bronte*. Penguin Books.

Gimbutas, Marija. *Gods and Goddesses of Old Rome: Myths and Cult Images*. Berkeley: University of California Press, 1987.

Gimbutas, Marija. *The Language of the Goddess*. San Francisco, CA: Harper & Row, 1989.

Gimbutas, Marija. *The Civilization of the Goddess*. San Francisco, CA: Harper & Collins, 1991.

Graves, Robert. *The Greek Myths*. Baltimore, MD: Penguin Books, 1955.

Graves, Robert. *The White Goddess*. NY: Farrar, Straus, & Giroux, 1948.

Harding, M. Esther. *Woman's Mysteries Ancient and Modern*. NY: Harper & Row, 1971.

Hungry Wolf, Beverly. *The Ways of My Grandmothers*. NY: Quill, 1982.

Jackson, Mildred. *Mental Birth Control*.

Kealoha, Anna. *Songs of the Earth*. Berkeley, CA: Celestial Arts, 1989.

Lacey, Louise. *Lunaception*. NY: Warner Books, 1975.

La Chapelle, Dolores. *Earth Festivals*. Silverton, CO: Finn Hill Arts, 1974.

La Chapelle, Dolores. *Sacred Land, Sacred Sex, Rapture of the Deep*. Silverton, CO: Finn Hill Arts, 1988.

La Pointe, James. *Legends of the Lakota*. San Francisco, CA: Indian Historical Press, 1976.

Mc Fadden, Steven. *Profiles in Wisdom: Native Elders Speak About the Earth*. Santa Fe, NM: Bear & Co., 1991.

Medicine Eagle, Brooke. *Buffalo Woman Comes Singing*. NY: Ballantine Books. 1991.

Monaghan, Patricia. *The Book of Goddesses and Heroines*. St. Paul, MN: Llewellyn Publications, 1990.

Niethammer, Carolyn. *Daughters of the Earth*. NY: Macmillan, 1977.

Nitsch, Twylah, and Sams, Jamie. *Other Council Fires Were Here Before Ours*. San Francisco: Harper & Collins, 1991.

Noble, Vicki. *Shakti Woman*. San Francisco, CA: Harper & Collins, 1991.

Parrinder, Geoffrey. *African Mythology*. NY: Peter Bedrick Books, 1982.

Rees, Alwyn, and Rees, Brinley. *Celtic Heritage*. Thames & Hudson, 1961.

Reichard, Gladys. *Navajo Religion*. Bollingen Series XVIII, Princeton, NJ: Princeton Univ. Press, 1970.

Rosenblum, Art. *The Natural Birth Control Book*. Philadelphia, PA: Aquarian Research Foundation, 1976.

Sams, Jamie. *Medicine Cards*. Santa Fe, NM: Bear & Co., 1988.

Sams, Jamie. *Sacred Path Cards*. San Francisco, CA: Harper & Collins, 1990.

Sjoo, Monica, and Mor, Barbara. *The Great Cosmic Mother*. San Francisco, CA: Harper & Row, 1987.

Starhawk. *The Spiral Dance*. San Francisco, CA: Harper & Row, 1979.

Stein, Diane. *Casting the Circle—A Women's Book of Ritual*. Freedom, CA: The Crossing Press, 1990.

Stein, Diane. *The Women's Spirituality Book*. St. Paul, MN: Llewellyn Publications, 1987.

Stephen, Alexander M. *Hopi Journal of Alexander M. Stephen*, ed. by Elsie C. Parsons. NY: Columbia Univ. Contributions to Anthropology, Vol. 23, 1936.

Stevenson, Matilda Cox. "The Zuni Indians." Bureau of American Ethnolology Anuual Report 23. Washington, DC: Smithsonian Institute, 1904.

Stone, Merlin. *Ancient Mirrors of Womanhood*. Boston, MA: Beacon Press, 1984.

Stone, Merlin. *When God Was a Woman*. NY: Harcourt Brace, 1976.

Taylor, G. Rattray. *Sex in History, Vol VI*. Thames & Hudson, 1953.

Teish, Luisah. *Jambalaya*. San Francisco, CA: Harper & Row, 1985.

Thorsten, Geraldine. *God Herself—The Feminine Roots of Astrology*. NY: Avon, 1980.

Walker, Barbara. *The Crone*. San Francisco, CA: Harper & Row, 1985.

Walker, Barbara. *The Woman's Encyclopedia of Myths and Secrets*. San Francisco, CA: Harper & Row, 1983.

Walker, Barbara. *Women's Rituals*. San Francisco, CA: Harper & Row, 1990.

Warner, Marina. *Alone of All Her Sex: The Myth and Cult of the Virgin Mary*. NY: Vintage Books, 1983.

Williamson, Ray A. *Living the Sky: The Cosmos of the American Indian*. Boston: Houghton Mifflin, 1984.

Wolfe, Amber. *In the Shadow of the Shaman*. St. Paul, MN: Llewellyn Publications, 1988.

Index

RELATED BOOKS BY THE CROSSING PRESS

Accupressure for Women
By Cathryn Bauer
$9.95 • Paper • 0-89594-232-1

All Women are Healers:
A Comprehensive Guide to Natural Healing
By Diane Stein
$14.95 • Paper • 0-89594-409-X

An Astrological Herbal for Women
By Elizabeth Brooke
$12.95 • Paper • 0-89594-740-4

Color and Crystals, A Journey Through the Chakras:
Healing with Color and Stones
By Joy Gardner-Gordon
$12.95 • Paper • 0-89594-258-5

Essential Reiki: A Complete Guide to an Ancient Healing Art
By Diane Stein
$18.95 · Paper · 0-89594-736-6

Healing with Gemstones and Crystals
by Diane Stein
$12.95 • Paper • 0-89594-831-1

Healing Yourself During Pregnancy
By Joy Gardner-Gordon
$12.95 • Paper • 0-89594-251-8

The Herbal Menopause Book:
Herbs, Nutrition, and Other Natural Remedies
By Amanda McQuade Crawford
$16.95 • Paper • 0-89594-799-4